WHAT EVERY MANAGER SHOULD KNOW ABOUT
SAFEGUARDING ADULTS AND CHILDREN

A HANDBOOK

Reg Pengelly

Grosvenor House
Publishing Limited

Independent Safeguarding Consultant
regpengelly@hotmail.com

This book is published by
Grosvenor House Publishing Ltd
28-30 High Street, Guildford, Surrey, GU1 3EL.
www.grosvenorhousepublishing.co.uk

A CIP record for this book
is available from the British Library

ISBN 978-1-78623-013-3

Reg Pengelly is the Independent Chair of the Local Safeguarding Children Board and the Local Safeguarding Adults Board for Bath and North East Somerset.

He was a senior police detective and a staff officer at the Home Office branch of Her Majesty's Inspectorate of Constabulary (HMIC). He represented HMIC at the Victoria Climbie Inquiry and led the police team that participated in the first joint Chief Inspector's National Inspection of Safeguarding Children. In 2003 he became the National Police Advisor on Child Protection and went on to help write national guidance on the investigation of child abuse, domestic violence and harrassment. In 2004 he joined the National Health Service and was the Associate Director responsible for safeguarding adults and children across Dorset, Bournemouth and Poole. He holds a number of management qualifications including a Masters Degree in Business Administration from the Henley Management College.

This short and practical guide builds on his previous book *What Every Manager Should Know About Safeguarding Children*. It has been written for the benefit of people who need to have an overview of this important subject, especially those in any organisation whose staff come into contact with adults in need of care and support or children and families.

Table of Contents

Introduction

This book is intended to summarise a vast body of legislation, guidance and information for the benefit of people who need an overview of this complex subject. The law and practice of safeguarding both children and adults is routinely subject to improvements and thus change is inevitable. It is well-nigh impossible to publish a book on this subject that is completely up to date. Indeed, at the time of publication of this book, the Government is considering the recommendations of a review into the role of Local Safeguarding Children Boards (LSCBs) and proposed new arrangements for the conduct of Serious Case Reviews.

To keep the information accessible, I have tried to maintain a conversational narrative and to that end I have been obliged to summarise particular subjects in a way that I hope does not detract from their importance. As a result, I have described certain individuals in a way that doesn't necessarily fit with current legislation, but I think will make more sense to the inexperienced. For example, where I make reference to 'vulnerable adults' or for that matter 'adults at risk', this should be taken to mean those adults who are in need of care or support (whether or not they are in receipt of those services). Similarly the terms 'vulnerable people' or 'the vulnerable' should be taken to mean vulnerable adults as well as children.

I have also used the acronym 'LADO' meaning the Local Authority Designated Officer. This description is no longer used in many Local Authorities but is nevertheless understood by safeguarding professionals to be the officer in a Local Authority who is nominated to coordinate multiagency work arising from allegations against people who work with children.

Similarly, although 'domestic abuse' is now the term preferred by most agencies, the terms 'domestic violence' and 'domestic violence and abuse' seem to be used interchangeably in much of the guidance that remains current.

High profile news stories about child abuse and the way in which an individual or an organisation has failed a child or a vulnerable adult are rarely absent from the national media. Whilst these often prompt useful debates about what should be changed, they rarely if ever highlight the extent to which abuse occurs in every locality. Regrettably at local levels, a belief persists that abuse is rare and when it occurs, it is committed by strangers. These are myths. Many adults and children die and many more suffer irreversible harm at the hands of their own family, or those whom society believes are best placed to care for them.

The term 'safeguarding' is largely accepted to mean protecting vulnerable people from maltreatment and preventing impairment of their health, circumstances or their development. For children in particular, it is about ensuring that they are growing up in circumstances consistent with the provision of safe and effective care. Thus the term can be used to describe both protective and preventative activity. It is an activity that takes place in a variety of different settings and at many levels.

In the context of protection, it is important to note that successful safeguarding is wholly reliant upon individual professionals assuming personal responsibility for taking action whenever they suspect abuse and following it up in a way appropriate to the circumstances.

Almost always, this will involve exchanging information with professionals from other agencies. The critical point here is that staff should receive training and ought to feel themselves empowered and supported by their organisation to assume this responsibility. The principal role of managers in this scenario, is to ensure that they are! One of the aims of this book is to provide an insight to managers as to how they can reconcile support and empowerment for staff with the business and constraints of their working environment.

Safeguarding is a complicated business. It exists within a framework of both criminal as well as civil law. Legislation is supported by a body of statutory guidance, much of which is the outcome of learning from the all too numerous public inquiries that have taken place from the second half of the twentieth century. To those unfamiliar with the tragic circumstances that led to these Inquiries, some of the guidance can appear to be somewhat draconian or perhaps odd. Regrettably it is all too easy for the sands of time to erode the learning upon which such guidance was orginally built. Arbitrarily or unwittingly ignoring this guidance on the basis that you think it to be inappropriate or excessive, is quite likely to put a child or adult at risk of continuing harm.

In support of the daily practice of dedicated safeguarding professionals, is a huge and ever expanding catalogue of research and practice guidance. Any manager who thinks that they can quickly read themselves into this particular portfolio and take unilateral decisions on reconfiguring a service, without reference to the expertise of their workforce and consultation with partners, is making a serious error of judgement.

The expertise of safeguarding professionals can easily be routinely ignored or undermined within organisations and even occasionally within the dialogue of Local Safeguarding Boards. Expertise in this field is borne out of passion, hard work and dedication. It is a valuable asset and needs to be readily available to all employees who come into contact with the vulnerable and needy in the course of their duties.

Whilst safeguarding professionals rarely have senior management experience, they have much to contribute in terms of assessing the multiagency impact of any proposed change. Ignoring the important contribution they can make to any relevant proposals is at best a serious blunder and at worst will put vulnerable people in the way of harm.

Quite rightly, there is a considerable body of legislation and guidance about the protection of personal information.

Medical professionals in particular, often feel themselves to be in a dilemma when confronted with an apparent concern, owing to the very strict rules about confidentiality that apply to health services. Similarly, much of the activity of other professionals is process driven with perceived limited authority to act outside of the process without reference to senior managers. For most organisations, the potential for substantial fines imposed by the Information Commissioner provide sufficient incentive to stifle communication.

It cannot be emphasised enough that where a concern about a vulnerable person arises, their welfare should ascend above all other considerations, including concerns about disclosing confidential information about the person, their carers, or for that matter anyone else implicated in arrangements for keeping them safe. In respect of children, this overriding principle is reflected both in the European Convention on Human Rights as well as the United Nations Convention on the Rights of the Child. Where any doubts arise about whether or not to exchange information in safeguarding, all professionals should feel empowered to take action on the basis of a genuine need to protect.

Abuse and neglect is unacceptable regardless of culture, religion, class, ideology and sexuality. In particular, respecting the rights of an adult is never an excuse for failing to protect a child.

Equally important is that in those circumstances that can be justifiably dealt with at a measured pace, advice should be available from a reliable and readily identifiable source. In health services this will be a Named or Designated Safeguarding Professional, in the Local Authority there will be a Children's or an Adult's Safeguarding Team, in the police service there will be a public protection function. Any other organisation or agency that does not have an 'in house' readily accessible safeguarding expert should be prepared to encourage their staff to contact the Local Authority Social Care team for advice whenever they need it.

I would like to acknowledge the practical support and helpful advice I have received from my wife Nicola throughout the process of writing this book. Particularly for sharing her extensive knowledge of domestic abuse and of multiagency workforce training arrangements.

Finally, I am also grateful to Liz Howarth, Roger Moore and their colleagues at the Virtual College who have kindly sponsored publication of this book.

CHAPTER ONE

Safeguarding Arrangements for Children

KEY POINTS

- Safeguarding operates within a legal framework in which key words are carefully defined.
- Safeguarding requires close cooperation and information sharing between professionals.
- The welfare of the child is always paramount.
- Children can be determined to be 'in need' or at 'risk of significant harm' as regulated by local thresholds.
- Timescales apply within the child protection process.

Definitions

What is a child?

For the purposes of the legislation relevant to this book, a child is someone who has not yet attained the age of 18 years.

Parental Responsibility (PR)

This is defined as all the rights, duties, powers, responsibilities and authority that by law, the parent of a child has in relation to that child. Parental responsibility can be shared by several people. The birth mother, unless the child has been adopted, always has PR. However the birth father may only have PR if married to the birth mother (either before or after the birth) or if since 2003, both parents registered the birth together. Otherwise, there are a variety of Court Orders that may define who has PR, such as Parental Responsibility Orders, Care Orders or Residence Orders.

The important point to note is that PR of a child should always be supported by evidence rather than assumption. Commonly this becomes an issue in circumstances of separation between parents where a father seeks access to a child in the care of a third party (e.g. a hospital or school) or to view the child's records held by a third party.

Competency and Consent

In the context of a variety of circumstances, legislation provides that children may be competent to consent to, or participate in, certain activities and may at different ages become criminally liable. For example, a child over 16 years may receive health services and will be entitled to confidentiality. In some circumstances where the child is considered to be sufficiently competent to understand the nature and consequences of a treatment, a child under 16 years may consent to receive some services confidentially. This includes sexual health services and contraception.

Managers should ensure that they and their staff have a full understanding of any legislation and guidance that sets out the age, competency and consent parameters pertaining to any services that are provided to children.

The Law – Children Acts 1989 and 2004

Much legislation and guidance exists to support the processes for safeguarding children and these are largely concerned with the rather complex relationships between agencies operating in a given local area. The principal legislation can be found in the Children Acts of 1989 and 2004 and the statutory guidance supporting this legislation is provided within *Working Together to Safeguard Children*.

The Children Act 1989 places at its core, the importance of working openly and collaboratively with families. Ideally, children are best protected by supporting parents to take good care of them. Similarly, children themselves have a right to know and should be helped to understand what is going on. Whenever practicable, children should be listened to throughout any process that concerns them and their views taken into account in any decisions that are taken.

Section 11 of the Children Act 2004 introduced the legal duty of many public sector organisations, to 'safeguard and promote the welfare of children'. Discharge of the duty is explained in some detail in *Working Together to Safeguard Children*. When these organisations commission services from others, they are also under a duty to ensure that anyone that provides a service on their behalf (usually because of a contract), also comply with Section 11. This should be a matter that is explicitly included in contracts and subject to clear contract governance arrangements.

The legislation and guidance consistently assert sole accountability for arrangements to safeguard and promote the welfare of children upon Chief Executives. Despite this, it is rare for Chief Executives to be held to account; except in the scenario of a Public Inquiry.

In defining what contributes to a child's well being, the Government produced a framework based on five essential outcomes. These are;

Stay Safe
Be Healthy
Make a Positive Contribution
Enjoy and Achieve
Achieve economic wellbeing

In the achievement of these outcomes, the development of an integrated multi-professional approach by relevant organisations is considered essential.

Types of Abuse and the Process for Protecting Children

Legislation describes the duties of agencies when;
(i)   a child is or may be at risk of significant harm; and
(ii) when a child is in need of support.

There are four categories of abuse. These are;

- Emotional
- Physical
- Sexual
- Neglect

There are more precise definitions of the categories and these are explained in a variety of documents and within the legislation. In recent years, abuse has been extended to include that of a child witnessing the abuse of another person, as in the case of a child witness to domestic abuse; who can be considered to have been emotionally harmed. This rather sensibly means that agendas for addressing domestic abuse should be inextricably linked to those for safeguarding children. More detailed information about this aspect is included later, particularly because domestic abuse is frequently encountered in every strata of society and is often a significant factor in a child becoming at risk of significant harm.

Children are at far more risk of abuse in their own homes than anywhere else. This includes the risk of sexual abuse. Furthermore there are a variety of risks to children that are very rarely within the public view. These are often complex and almost exclusively only understood by professionals who have been trained in safeguarding. An example is that in which a parent or carer will present an apparently sick child for medical attention. The symptoms will have been fabricated or induced by the parent or carer and often they will exacerbate these symptoms during the course of diagnosis and treatment. All Local Safeguarding Children Boards are expected to have procedures in place to coordinate the activity of agencies to address these special risks.

Child Sexual Exploitation

Child Sexual Exploitation (CSE) has become a highly topical issue in recent years following public revelations of decades of sexual predation on the part of celebrities and people in high office. More recently, prolific sexual exploitation has been uncovered in a number of towns and cities. It is clear that this too has taken place over many years and has apparently evaded the surveillance of those charged with the reponsibility of protection.

Research and investigations have revealed that girls and boys, continue to be systematically targeted and groomed to submit themselves to such abuse. This may be in the context of a gravitational pull into the activities of gangs in which girls are soon routinely shared for sex between gang members, or of girls and boys being initially befriended and subsequently prostituted within the control of organised criminals.

Whilst Internet social networking plays a significant part in facilitating initial contact, many children are just as likely to become groomed through personal street contact with men and women who befriend them. Ultimately children who are subject to these activities will find it almost impossible to extricate themselves without external intervention, such as a police operation and will often require dedicated long term therapies to recover. Regrettably the availability of such support, especially in terms of mental health therapies, is often in short supply.

Local multiagency activity to address CSE includes the use of CSE Panels, in which the particular risks faced by individual children are discussed and a plan to divert and support them is formulated. This can be used for children who are thought to be at risk of becoming victims as well as those who have already become so. Early indications of children who may be particularly susceptible to CSE include being regularly missing from home or care, poor school attendance, involvement in or within the periphery of gang activities, substance misuse and self-harm. In this context, CSE might be considered a legitimate issue for Public Health services.

Abuse of Disabled Children

Disabled children, being children already 'in need', represent a significant number of the total child population and are disproportionately at a higher risk of abuse and neglect. These are children with difficulties that range from physical, sensory and learning disabilities to chronic illness and significant mental health problems.

The principle that 'the welfare of the child is paramount' applies in these circumstances more starkly than in most others. The parent or carer's concerns and expectations must never override protection of the child.

The Child Protection Process

The following narrative provides a summary of how multiagency child protection happens. Understanding the process will allow managers in particular, to determine how their organisation is best placed to respond when a concern about a child arises.

The child may as a result of their circumstances, be in need of support. Two levels of support are described in the Children Act 1989. These are in respect of 'a child in need' or of 'a child suffering or likely to suffer significant harm'.

The definition of a 'child in need' " is very wide. Of critical importance is that a thorough assessment leading to the identification of effective interventions takes place. Many children 'in need' can become 'children at risk of significant harm' as a result of a more detailed assessment or because of a deterioration in their circumstances or an escalation of abuse.

There are no objective criteria on which to rely when judging what constitutes significant harm. Under S31 (10) of the Children Act 2004, the question of whether harm suffered by a child is 'significant' relates specifically to the child's health and development. Their health or development should be compared with that which could reasonably be expected of a similar child and the parenting that we would reasonably expect them to receive from their parent/carer.

To understand and identify significant harm, it is necessary to consider:

–   the nature of harm, in terms of mistreatment or failure to provide adequate care;
–   the impact on the child's health and development;

- the child's development within the context of their family and wider environment;
- any special needs, such as a medical condition, communication impairment or disability, that may affect the child's development and care within the family;
- the capacity of parents to adequately meet the child's needs; and
- the wider family and environmental context.

Where a child is found to be at risk of significant harm, *Working Together to Safeguard Children* mandates a process for managing the case and this includes the role of agencies that may become involved, and how their involvement should take place. For example, where a crime against a child may have taken place, the police should be informed immediately and they in turn are required to engage within the process so that their criminal investigation is coordinated with the activity of other agencies to safeguard the child.

The Children's Services Authority (often described as 'Children's Services' and within which a Children's Social Care function operates) at the top tier of Local Government (e.g. a Unitary or County Council), is legally empowered and accountable to act as the central hub for all operational safeguarding activity for children.

It is important to keep in mind that the concept of Children's Services as the hub, is not simply the legislative position, since all safeguarding activity is coordinated from here, but also that it serves a very practical function that is best placed to take the lead in safeguarding activity. It will include a dedicated social work team for out of hours advice and support. However you should note that (where it functions in this regard) a Multi Agency Safeguarding Hub (MASH) may be the point of receipt for referals or concerns according to local arrangements.

In the first instance, all referrals or concerns about a child should be routed to this hub, in line with local arrangements. By this means, the information provided may be viewed in a broader context of knowledge about the child, their family or other circumstances.

There is a tiered approach to making assessments of need when such referrals are made, alongside timescales for getting these completed. Where appropriate, strategy discussions take place between the professionals involved and further meetings may take place that may eventually lead to a child protection conference, in which a plan for safeguarding the child is agreed, acted upon and monitored.

In very urgent circumstances, the police have powers to remove a child to safety and there is provision for securing emergency care arrangements for children from the Courts. In appropriate circumstances, Social Workers may lawfully seek consent from parents or carers to remove their child into care.

By far the most contentious aspect of the multiagency safeguarding process is that of thresholds. There are many facets in determining which cases conclude that a child is in need or at risk of significant harm. Similarly, there are degrees in the level of risk. This is a matter of judgement based on local procedures within the Children's Services team. In some cases referrals will not qualify for the next tier of assessment.

These arrangements amount to what is commonly perceived as a gatekeeping exercise, which critics argue is more informed by staff capacity than meeting a child's needs robustly. Staff from other agencies are often extremely frustrated when they feel that this is the case and the outcome in terms of interagency relationships has in my experience, occasionally become rather frosty. For example, many front line health professionals such as health visitors and school nurses, signal that they are often managing a much higher level of risk for children in their caseloads because cases that might once have been considered to require Social Care intervention are now not reaching that threshold and fall to the referring professional to manage.

It is incredibly difficult to measure whether there is any truth to this popular belief but what is very clear is that nationally, safeguarding caseloads amongst these health professionals have increased significantly. It is equally evident that the number of children that do meet the threshold for child protection plans has also increased and that because of this, the caseloads of Children's Services staff has grown with it.

All managers need to be aware of the dangers that thresholds present for relationships between professionals. Interagency communication and strong interpersonal relationships are a critical factor in managing this particular risk. LSCBs have a role in promoting and supporting such relationships and should always be consulted when thresholds are to be amended.

The Multiagency Conference and Timescales

Working Together to Safeguard Children prescribes some timescales for activities that support the child protection process. In some areas these have been adjusted to suit local processes and circumstances. Thus they should be confirmed by reference to local procedures published by the Local Safeguarding Children Board. The following is an abbreviated summary taken from the perspective of a referring agency. There are many other functions or options that may be undertaken by Children's Services to support the process.

More often than not, the initial communication that a child is suspected to be at risk of significant harm, is made verbally. This should be followed up by way of a formal written report or letter from the referrer. This report or written referral form, is often prepared using an agreed multiagency template made available by local Children's Social Care.

The social worker allocated the case must acknowledge receipt of the referral and decide how to respond to it based on an assessment of all the facts known at the time. This may lead to one of a number of decisions as to whether;

- the child requires immediate protection and urgent action is needed;
- the child is in need and should be assessed under Section 17 of the Children Act 1989;

- there is reasonable cause to suspect that the child is suffering or is likely to suffer significant harm and whether enquiries must be made including an assessment of the child under Section 47 of the Children Act 1989;
- whether any services are required by the child and family and what type of services; and
- whether any further specialist assessments are required in order to help the Local Authority determine what further action it should take.

Note that the child and family should ordinarily be advised of any decisions that affect them unless doing so might place a child at risk of harm.

If the Social Worker confirms that the referral amounts to a concern that a child is or may be at risk of significant harm, this will trigger enquiries pursuant to Section 47 Children Act 1989, typically described as 'a Section 47 case', (meaning that it is a significant harm inquiry).

Where the referral is considered to amount to such a concern, a strategy discussion between the relevant agencies will take place in which the decision to pursue a Section 47 case will be confirmed and the next steps to be taken are planned and coordinated.

Where emergency action needs to be taken, for example an urgent care application; such action should normally take place following a strategy discussion involving appropriate agencies. However, at any stage where a child might be at immediate risk of significant harm, urgent and sometimes unilateral action may be taken.

Strategy discussions between relevant agencies may take place at any time as appropriate to the progression of the case. These could be formal meetings or telephone calls. However, the Chair of the meeting should circulate notes of what was discussed to all participants within one working day.

An initial assessment should take place as soon as possible after the date of the referral. This may lead to identification of the child as 'in need' and in turn that might lead to preparation of a multiagency assessment in which the child's particular needs are explored more fully. A multiagency assessment is a very detailed piece of work that requires careful planning and can take several weeks to complete. The assessment is supposed to be completed within 45 days and agencies have a duty to assist this process by the timely provision of relevant information.

Where the initial assessment confirms the child to be at risk, a child protection conference must be held within 15 working days of the initial strategy discussion at which the Section 47 enquiries are commenced. It is important that any professionals involved in the case who have a relevant contribution to make and are so invited, should attend this conference in person even if they have previously submitted a written report. This invitation is unavoidably, often made at relatively short notice.

All organisations who have staff in respect of whom such short notice invitations may be made, should have robust arrangements in place for resilience or contingency cover that facilitates attendance. Failure to attend such a meeting when invited to do so, should only be considered an acceptable option when it is completely unavoidable and due to circumstances beyond the control of your organisation.

Staff attending the conference will be required to participate in the risk assessment based on their own and other information shared there. If a manager is concerned that an employee may be insufficiently experienced in this part of the conference, they should arrange to attend with them and should make time to talk the case through with the employee beforehand. This aspect also highlights the importance of a sound training experience for staff.

The child protection conference will;

- share relevant information about the child and family;
- assess the risk to the child;
- decide whether the child is at continuing risk of significant harm;
- decide whether the actions required to safeguard and promote the welfare of the child need to be formulated within the framework of a child protection plan;
- appoint a key worker who must be a social worker or a nominee from the NSPCC;
- identify membership of the core group who will develop and implement the plan;
- ensure a contingency plan is in place if agreed actions are not completed and/or circumstances change and
- agree about if and when to reconvene and review progress.

The child, subject to their age and understanding, may attend the conference and may bring an advocate or supporter with them. Parents and carers are usually encouraged to attend and advised to seek legal advice or an advocate as necessary. This experience can be as intimidating for inexperienced professionals as it is for the parents.

It is likely that a multiagency assessment will not be completed at this stage. The main decisions of a conference should be shared within one working day although detailed notes of the conference will take much longer to prepare. Individual agencies are expected to keep records of conferences and this includes health records for the family and child, which are normally held by their GP.

An outline child protection plan will be agreed at the initial conference; however a Core Group will be appointed to develop a more detailed child protection plan. The parents are likely to be included in the Core Group as is the child; subject to their age or competency. The focus of the Core Group should be upon the outcomes that will improve things for the child rather than upon the specific actions. The first meeting of the Core Group must take place within 10 working days of the initial child protection conference.

A record is maintained by the Local Authority of all children who are subject to Child Protection Plans. Safeguarding professionals in agencies including those in health services, may by local arrangement, be able to check whether children are subject to plans (often cited as 'on the register', an expression persisting since a time predating the latest Children Act). This check will ensure that any information relevant to the continuing safety of the child is made known to the professional seeing the child and if appropriate, any fresh information is in turn passed to the Local Authority.

The first child protection review conference must be held within three months of the initial conference. The review conference requires the same level of commitment as the initial conference and it is essential that relevant professionals attend in person. Except when a child becomes an adult at 18 years, or when the family moves to another area (where responsibility for the plan will be passed to a new team), the review conference is the only authority for discontinuing a child protection plan.

There will always be a range of seriousness in which some child in need cases and some significant harm cases are separated, often merely on a judgement call by the assessing professional. Managers should ensure that the categorisation of a case does not automatically result in a reduction in the vigilance and engagement of those professionals working with the child and the family. It will always be necessary to reconsider what the categorisation means in terms of their particular needs. Regrettably, many agencies have in the past, as a matter of routine, stepped down their level of engagement in the absence of a child protection plan or on learning that a case has been assessed to amount to a child in need. In this way children have been left exposed to harm and on occasions, have died as a result.

Looked After Children

From the child's perspective, the outcome of child protection processes might result in a Court determining
that they should be subject to temporary fostering
arrangements, a stay in a Local Authority care facility, or
adoption. Children who have not been adopted but
remain under the responsibility of the Local Authority
by virtue of a Court Order or who in temporary or emergency circumstances, are under protection are usually
described as 'Looked After Children'.

Children in these circumstances are extremely vulnerable
and often require substantial practical support from
a number of agencies. This support needs to be well-
planned with active participation from the child wherever practicable. Oversight of the continuing welfare of
looked after children is the responsibility of the Local
Authority.

A substantial body of guidance has evolved about the
role of agencies in supporting looked after children and
this is routinely subject to inspection and local scrutiny.
NHS services should appoint a specialist nurse to coordinate health support. Above all, the support to looked
after children should be integrated into the way that
each agency delivers services. It should not be seen as a
specialist role and much less something entirely within
the remit of a specialist safeguarding service.

The Common Assessment Framework

Assessments of children whose support needs fall short of
child protection arrangements, may utilise the 'Common

Assessment Framework'. The CAF as it is more commonly known, helps professionals to identify the most effective support for a family, and facilitates multiagency collaboration. An assessment can be completed at any time it is believed that a child will not be able to progress towards the five essential outcomes.

The CAF is a four-step process whereby practitioners can identify a child's or young person's needs early, assess those needs holistically, deliver coordinated services and review progress.

STEP 1 - IDENTIFY NEEDS EARLY
STEP 2 - ASSESS THOSE NEEDS
STEP 3 - DELIVER INTEGRATED SERVICES
STEP 4 - REVIEW PROGRESS

The CAF is designed to be used when a practitioner is worried about how well a child or young person is progressing (e.g. concerns about their health, development, welfare, behaviour, progress in learning or any other aspect of their wellbeing) a child or young person, or their parent or carer, raises a concern with a practitioner, a child's or young person's needs are unclear, or broader than the practitioner's service can address.

The process is entirely voluntary and informed consent is mandatory, so families do not have to engage and if they do they can choose what information they want to share. Children and families should not feel stigmatised by the CAF; indeed they can ask for a CAF to be initiated at any time.

The CAF process is not a referral process but a request for services. The CAF should be offered to children who have additional needs to those that could be met by universal services. Thus unless a child requires additional services, it is unlikely the CAF will be appropriate. The CAF should not be used as a risk assessment. If a child or young person reveals they are at risk of harm, the practitioner should follow the local child protection procedures immediately.

There can be an unrealistic expectation that a trained Social Worker will always undertake the CAF or will always lead the work to support a child in need or their family. This responsibility will more usually fall to the practitioner who instigated the original referral, provided they are sufficiently competent.

Since a large proportion of children in need are identified by frontline professionals it is important that operational managers are alert to staff workloads and should ensure that support, supervision and professional advice is provided. I cannot overemphasise the importance of managers maintaining awareness of the implications of this aspect of safeguarding upon the capacity of their staff. A workload of this kind can be overwhelming in terms of personal capacity and their emotional welfare.

Early Help

The concept of Early Help is promoted as being more effective in promoting the welfare of children than reacting later. Early Help means providing support as soon as a problem arises at any point in a child's life. To be effective it relies upon local agencies working together to identify, assess and provide targeted support. To that end Local Safeguarding Children Boards are tasked with responsibility for monitoring the effectiveness of Early Help.

The most important action that a manager can take where such chidren may be in the care of their organisation or where services are provided to the child or family, is to recognise the very real risk of abuse and to take steps to mitigate these. Supervision is discussed later in this book and is a very important protective factor in these circumstances. Further guidance on this topic is included in the list of documents in the Further Reading section at the end of this book.

CHAPTER TWO

The Local Safeguarding Children Board

> **KEY POINTS**
>
> - The LSCB oversees how local agencies safeguard and promote the welfare of children through coordination and scrutiny.
> - Certain agencies are under a legal duty to engage with the LSCB.
> - The LSCB may initiate a Serious Case Review (SCR) into the involvement of agencies where a child has died or is seriously harmed.
> - Agencies are expected to respond to the learning from SCR. This may involve fundamental changes to the way they are managed.

Scope and Remit

Local Safeguarding Children Boards (LSCB) were established as a result of the Children Act 2004. Previously, similar functions were undertaken by bodies known as Area Child Protection Committees (ACPC).

The significant diffence between the ACPC and LSCB is that the latter includes the coordination and monitoring of safeguarding activity as well as protection.

It is worth reflecting that many of the arrangements for safeguarding that were included in the 2004 Act arose as a direct result of the Victoria Climbie Inquiry, conducted by Lord Laming. I mention this because the findings of that inquiry demonstrated more than any other, that safeguarding children should be everyone's business and not just that of the Local Authority Children's Social Care team. Establishment of LSCBs within a legal framework of partnership was a major advance. Many public sector organisations are under a statutory duty to cooperate with the LSCB by virtue of the Children Act 2004.

LSCBs have a legal responsibility to oversee multiagency safeguarding arrangements and to hold partner agencies (i.e. those under a duty to cooperate) to account for their contribution to those arrangements. Agencies under a legal duty to cooperate with the LSCB include the police, health services, relevant local authorities, departments such as Children's Services, education, housing, and Probation Services and all of these should be represented on the Board by senior (executive) level managers. Other organisations may be invited to take part in the Board and often they will include representatives from the voluntary sector, local armed services and lay members representing the community.

It is usual for LSCBs to take responsibility for organising or at least promoting local safeguarding training, the development of joint policies and protocols, as well as assuring the quality of work undertaken through audits and reviews. LSCBs also have specific legal duties in the organisation of Serious Case Reviews and the Child Death Review process. These functions will be descibed later.

Funding for LSCBs is likely to be drawn through contributions made by the partner agencies although there is no legal compulsion for them to do so and there is no central funding provided either. In recent times, LSCBs have been obliged to appoint Independent Chairs to their Boards. Independent Chairs are paid for their services either as employees of the Local Authority or as contractors.

There are many variations on a theme in the way that LSCBs function and often this will be influenced by the personal approach of the Independent Chair. Ideally, the LSCB will have the means to monitor how well or otherwise safeguarding activity is conducted within its area and will set out a clear plan for the year's activities in terms of promoting safeguarding and will monitor progress at Board meetings. In addition, all LSCBs will have the means to quality assure their local safeguarding arrangements.

The work of the LSCB is invariably distributed between a number of subgroups and each LSCB will have their own way of doing things. Of the manifold functions undertaken by LSCBs, two are legal requirements. These concern the establishment of Serious Case Reviews (or audits) and a process for reviewing all child deaths.

Serious Case Reviews and Audits

There remains room for considerable debate about the effectiveness of Serious Case Reviews as a vehicle for improvement. These reviews are essentially investigations into the reasons for a failure of local arrangements that has led to the death of, or serious injury to a child. Until recently, they have followed a highly prescriptive process that was rather bureaucratically followed by an evaluation overseen by Ofsted.

Many critics have claimed that the process became more important than the outcome of such reviews and cite that in many areas, consecutive reviews have found the same mistakes being made time and time again with no signs of learning having resulted in improvement. A substantial review of safeguarding conducted by Professor Eileen Munroe fuelled the debate further and in turn has led to exploration of alternative approaches to the concept of learning from past mistakes.

Even given new approaches towards less beauracratic serious case reviews, they remain extremely expensive undertakings, with the services of an Independent Author and a Panel Chair often costing in the region of £10 – £20,000. These costs are borne within the LSCB budget and should be reclaimed or allowed for, through partner agency contributions. Additionally there will be opportunity cost to organisations undertaking Individual Management Reviews (IMR) and incurred through providing staff to support the conduct of the LSCB Panel that oversees activity. Given the labour and expense of such undertakings, it is both wasteful and depressing to find that learning is not always translated into improvement that makes a difference.

Traditionally, Serious Case Reviews and where appropriate, Serious Case Audits have comprised of two components; IMR reports and a final Overview Report. The IMR is the report of a review that has been conducted internally within a single agency and the overview report brings together the findings of all constituent IMRs and in this context attempts to make sense of any interagency activity that has taken place.

More recently a third kind of report has been introduced called the Health Overview Report (HOR). This acknowlededes the complex interrelationships between different health providers such as Hospitals, General Practitioners, Dentists etc, bringing together the collection of health service IMRs in support of the subsequent delivery of a final Overview Report. It is usual that HOR will be prepared by the Designated Nurse covering the health area associated with the LSCB.

The structure and content of both kinds of report has up until recently been required to fit a prescribed format but is now much less regimented. However both types of report require the construction of a chronology of significant events, careful reconstruction of relevant facts and analysis of the quality of practice revealed, by reference to research and professional standards. Managers required to undertake IMR should be experienced in the field of safeguarding so that they are best placed to identify critical issues in the chronology and can apply relevant standards and research to their findings.

The intention of these reviews is to facilitate learning so that any mistakes are not repeated. The reviews are explicitly not intended as disciplinary investigations, although it should be acknowledged that from time to time, serious breaches of professional conduct are discovered and this will lead to a separate but parallel investigation.

Her Majesty's Government has made it an absolute requirement upon LSCBs to publish the full report of a Serious Case Review. The only exception (in the opinion of LSCB Chairs), is where publication might in itself harm a child. A National Panel has been established to oversee how LSCBs manage SCRs and to scrutinise any decisions regarding publication.

LSCBs are required by *Working Together to Safeguard Children*, to develop a Learning and Development Framework. This document should describe the means by which the LSCB ensures that learning from audits and reviews, not only from its own area but also from other sources, is integrated into the improvement of practice. This should be geared to assure better outcomes for children and families. The Learning and Improvement Framework should be a dynamic document that evolves with the ever changing landscape of service and workforce redesign.

Different approaches to reviewing cases have been implemented as a result of Professor Munroe's review of safeguarding arrangements. Practitioner's feedback of their experience of participating in these reviews has been very positive. A key difference is that the reviewers produce a list of findings rather than specific recommendations and it is for the LSCB to determine how to respond.

However the implementation of improvement will always remain a challenge to LSCBs and member organisations. An even greater challenge is for organisations, both those participating in LSCBs and others that provide services for children and families, to proactively improve their safeguarding so that the potential for these mistakes is limited from the outset.

In March 2016, the Government received the recommendations of a review of LSCBs and of the conduct of Serious Case Reviews. At the time of writing, it is now considering how to respond and it is likely that at the least, those case reviews of particularly heinious or highly significant abuse may become centrally managed rather than by their 'host' LSCBs.

A synopsis of the findings from all SCRs in England and Wales is published every two years. Here again, as reflected in these national Biennial Reviews, many mistakes are continually repeated with little or no sign of an enduring commitment to improve things. Given that these reviews often highlight the significance of prevention rather than cure, the lack of improved outcomes for children and families is rather disappointing.

Biennial and the more recent Triennial Reviews have repeatedly identified;

- neglect is a background factor in the majority of cases for children of all ages;

- confirmation of the importance of universal services, including schools;
- the primary years present the best opportunities for prevention;
- a need for more understanding of risks associated with parental separation;and
- confirmation of the importance of supervision.

Child Death Reviews

Working Together to Safeguard Children provides the statutory framework for processes in relation to reviewing childhood deaths. The deaths of all children normally resident in the LSCB area are collectively subject to the scrutiny of a local Child Death Overview Panel (CDOP). Note that this would include deaths of local children that take place overseas e.g. whilst on holiday.

Statutory Regulations require LSCBs to establish procedures both to respond rapidly to individual unexpected childhood deaths and to review all childhood deaths in a systematic way. Unxexpected deaths should be subject to a rapid response and if appropriate a home visit, jointly between trained clinicians and the police. The approach taken in rapid response will be commensurate with the particular circumstances of each case.

Unexpected child deaths are subject to a local review soon after they have taken place, usually led by a senior paediatrician. In many areas the CDOP has elected for all child deaths (i.e. unexpected and expected) to be subject to local reviews.

The core responsibilities of the Child Death Overview Panel are as follows:

(a) To collect and analyse information about each death with a view to identifying;

- any case giving rise to the need for a Serious Case Review;
- any matters of concern affecting the welfare of children in the area of the authority; and
- any wider public health or safety concerns arising from a particular death or from a pattern of deaths in that area.

(b) To put into place procedures for ensuring that there is a co-ordinated response by the authority, their Board partners and other relevant persons to an unexpected death.

The above list demonstrates that in meeting these responsibilities, there are a large number of processes that the CDOP and the LSCB to which it is subsumed should follow. Supporting these processes are a number of nationally developed forms that underpin both local activity and the collection of national data about childhood deaths.

Given that childhood deaths are mercifully small in number, this also means that at a local level, numbers are often too few to develop the evidence from which much, if any worthwhile preventative activity could be justified. For this and a number of other practical reasons, many LSCBs have combined their CDOP function so that a single CDOP might cover several LSCB areas.

Feedback about the experience of bereaved families is also very useful as this may inform the development of improvements to services or even new ones. This latter point is especially important when considering both the needs of recently bereaved parents as well as the perspectives of minority cultures. Any deficiencies should become a matter of continuing scrutiny for both the CDOP and the LSCB until they are resolved.

Because child deaths may not be reviewed by the CDOP for quite a number of months, it is important that commissioners and providers of services are sighted on any learning from the more immediate perspective of local child death reviews. This will ensure that improvement is driven at the earliest opportunity. Thus it is important that managers responsible for quality and safety in agencies maintain connections with the findings of local child death reviews as well as the CDOP.

Quality Assurance Functions of LSCBs

The LSCB should provide local oversight of the way that children are safeguarded. This is not simply oversight of the child protection system but should include other aspects that affect the welfare of children too. This is not to suggest that the LSCB should duplicate the work of other bodies; such as for example any local Children's Trust arrangements or the work of the Health and Well-being Boards. But the LSCB should be certain that these bodies are indeed holding local agencies to account in respect of the panoply of aspects that affect children's welfare and are able to confirm that there are no gaps in provision.

One important aspect of LSCB oversight should be an audit of all relevant organisations in terms of their discharge of the statutory duty to safeguard and promote the welfare of children under Section 11, Children Act 2004. There are a number of ways to achieve this and many LSCBs already conduct such an audit annually.

LSCBs may also develop a local data set so that the Board may routinely monitor the performance of agencies and aspects of safeguarding that it believes will provide a perspective on how well children's welfare is promoted. This data at one level is likely to include information about the number of children who are subject to child protection plans, the number of Section 47 referrals received from each agency and the number of children taken into care.

At another level the data may show a richer perspective, for example, in the domain of children and domestic abuse, how many children are to be found in domestic abuse refuges, how long they have to wait to be placed in school and how long they wait to be rehoused. Not much if any of this however, tells the LSCB about the child's experience. The really effective LSCBs will have the wherewithall to obtain feedback directly from children and families about their experiences.

It is likely that all LSCBs will have a subgroup or committee responsible for quality assurance functions. Sometimes this responsibility may be divided between two or more groups depending on the type of assurance required. For example, LSCBs should ensure that the recommendations of Serious Case Reviews are followed up and this particular function may fall to a Serious Case Review Panel.

Above and beyond that function, the LSCB should have a group responsible for routine audits of performance which may be thematic or in the form of sampling exercises or perhaps a combination of the two. Such audits may be in the form of file reading exercises or may take the form of a local review meeting in which a number of cases are taken together with the relevant practitioners. For the reasons previously discussed, the purpose is to achieve learning from all of this, and most importantly that the learning drives tangible improvements for the lives of children and families.

CHAPTER THREE

Safeguarding Adults

KEY POINTS

- Safeguarding applies to adults who are in need of services or support whether or not they are in receipt of them.
- An extensive list of types of abuse is applicable to adults. This includes self-harm.
- Adults are entitled to exercise choice throughout.
- Decisions made on behalf of adults who do not have the mental capacity to do so for themselves must be made in their best interests.
- Legal protections apply when adults are subjected to any deprivation of their liberty.

Safeguarding adults is about protecting the vulnerable in our communities. The majority of us are more than capable of protecting ourselves from exploitation and harm. We have clear choices and on those occasions when we become victims of violence, crime, accident or our own folly, a variety of remedies may be accessible to us.

In the context of people aged 18 years and over, the Care Act 2014 describes criteria for determining whether an adult is appropriate to be considered for safeguarding. Firstly they should be in need of community services by reason of mental or other disability, their age or an illness (whether they are actually in receipt of services is irrelevant for this test). Secondly that they are experiencing or are at risk of abuse or neglect AND they are unable to protect themselves from the harm or exploitation or the risk of it.

This definition makes a significant and sensible alteration to a previous definition, in that prior to the Care Act, the person in need had to be actually in receipt of services. This of course means that many more people can be considered to be in need of safeguarding than hitherto. It should also be noted that where a person over 18 years remains in receipt of children's services (often but not exclusively by reason of disability), the adult, (not children's) safeguarding arrangements would apply to them.

The six key principles of adult safeguarding

All adult safeguarding work should be underpinned by the following principles;

- Empowerment
- Prevention
- Proportionality
- Protection
- Partnership
- Accountability

These principles are implicit throughout the Care Act. They are especially relevant to the concept of wellbeing, explained below;

Wellbeing

Wellbeing, in relation to an adult is really about their quality of life and specifically refers to any of the following;

- personal dignity (including treatment of the individual with respect);
- physical and mental health and emotional wellbeing;
- protection from abuse and neglect;
- control by the individual over day-to-day life (including over care and support, or support, provided to the individual and the way in which it is provided);
- participation in work, education, training or recreation;
- social and economic wellbeing;
- domestic, family and personal relationships;
- suitability of living accommodation; and
- the individual's contribution to society.

Choice and Capacity

A significant safeguarding consideration relevant to adults is that they are presumed to have greater choice in how to live their lives than children. This includes the choice to do things or take decisions that, to others might seem stupid or even reckless. (Always providing that the person has full command of their mental faculties when taking such a decision, or in safeguarding terms, that they have 'mental capacity'.)

Special arrangements apply whenever an adult is thought not to have mental capacity and if the arrangements are applicable, this does not necessarily mean that their entitlement to make choices is completely removed. This aspect will be explored later, but it should be borne in mind throughout this section, that adults considered for safeguarding arrangements have a choice in any safeguarding process and are entitled to refuse help at any stage.

The Purpose of Safeguarding Adults

For adults, the purpose of safeguarding is to promote their independence and wellbeing by supporting and empowering them to prevent and manage the risk of harm. In doing so the adult should always know that they are in control of what happens and that safeguarding responds to what they want, rather than what others think they need.

Organisations should always promote the adult's wellbeing in their safeguarding arrangements. People lead complex lives and have many personal aspirations and differing perspectives. Being safe is only one of the things they want for themselves. Professionals should work with the adult to establish what being safe means to them and how that can best be achieved. Professionals and other staff should never advocate safety measures that do not take account of individual wellbeing.

Making Safeguarding Personal

Aligned with implementation of the Care Act is the drive to ensure that adults in receipt of support have control over what happens. *Making Safeguarding Personal* demands a person centred and outcome focussed approach. Through this approach, the adult is engaged throughout in a conversation about how best to respond to their safeguarding needs in a way that enhances involvement, choice and control as well as improving quality of life, wellbeing and safety.

For many professionals this way of working has demanded a rethink of their working practice. Personal choice is a key theme throughout the Care Act and no less so within the context of safeguarding. This will include supporting adults to think and weigh up the risks and benefits of different options when exercising choice and control. It is about seeing people as experts in their own lives and working alongside them. Just as importantly it is about collecting information about the extent to which this shift of perspective has a positive impact on people's lives.

Ultimately *Making Safeguarding Personal* is a shift from a process supported by conversations to a series of conversations supported by a process.

Proportionality

Because children have so little choice in what is decided in their best interests, a principle of paramouncy applies in their safeguarding arrangements. This means that whenever any conflict of interest arises in safeguarding a child, the child's welfare is held to be paramount, even if this entails risks for others or means that the child is removed from their family environment against their wishes.

For adults, there is a subtle but important difference. Safeguarding arrangements for adults need to recognise that the right to safety should be balanced with other rights such as rights to liberty and autonomy and rights to family life. For example, while abusive relationships can never contribute to the wellbeing of an adult, interventions which remove all contact with family members may also be considered to be an abusive intervention and might risk breaching the adults right to family life if the intervention is not justified and proportional.

Safeguarding and Safety

Safeguarding means protecting an adult's right to live in safety, free from abuse and neglect. Keeping people safe requires carers, staff and organisations to collaborate. Adults can be ambivalent, unclear or unrealistic about their personal circumstances and this should be recognised throughout. Organisations must always promote the adult's wellbeing in their safeguarding arrangements. However these duties should not be seen as a substitute for;

- providing safe and high quality care and support;
- the obligation upon commissioners to assure themselves of the safety and effectiveness of services they commission;
- the work of regulators such as the Care Quality Commission ensuring compliance with standards of care; or
- the core duties of the police to protect life and property and to prevent and detect crime.

Infrastructure

The Local Authority is obliged to establish an infrastructure for safeguarding and the Care Act places local Health Services and the Police under a duty to cooperate in these arrangements. The arrangements require the Local Authority to;

- make enquiries or cause others to do so, if it believes an adult is experiencing or is at risk of abuse or neglect;
- establish a Local Safeguarding Adults Board (LSAB) comprising representation from the local Clinical Commissioning Group (CCG), the police and any other members deemed necessary for the LSAB to carry out its functions;
- arrange as appropriate for independent advocacy to support adults in safeguarding enquiries who are unable to represent themselves and who cannot be represented by any other suitable person of their choice; and
- cooperate with relevant partners to protect the adult. (In their turn partners are required to cooperate.)

Whilst the CCG and police are required to participate in the establishment of a LSAB, in the broader context of safeguarding a larger group of partner organisations are under a duty to cooperate with the Local Authority. These include the CCG and Police but also NHS England, NHS Trusts and Foundation Trusts, the Department for Work and Pensions, Prisons, the National Probation Service and Community Rehabilitation Companies. In particular circumstances, the Local Authority must cooperate with other agencies or bodies such as (and not limited to) General Practitioners, dentists, housing providers, Fire and Rescue Services and Armed Services.

The Aims of Safeguarding for Adults

The aims of any safeguarding activity are described in the statutory guidance as to;

- stop abuse or neglect wherever possible;
- prevent harm and reduce the risk of abuse or neglect to adults with care and support needs;
- safeguard adults in a way that supports them in making choices and having control about how they want to live;
- promote an approach that concentrates on improving life for the adults concerned;
- raise public awareness so that communities as a whole, alongside professionals, play their part in preventing, identifying and responding to abuse and neglect;
- provide information and support in an accessible way to help people understand the different types of abuse, how to stay safe and what to do to raise a concern about the safety or wellbeing of an adult; and
- address what has caused the abuse or neglect.

Types of Abuse and Neglect

The first point is that Local Authorities should not limit their view of what constitutes abuse or neglect. The circumstances of each case should be considered in the context of how the Care Act outlines who safeguarding is applicable to. This means that the following list should be considered a guide and not a definitive demarcation;

- **Physical Abuse.** This might include assault, misuse of medication, restraint or inappropriate physical sanctions.
- **Domestic Abuse.** Including coercive control, psychological, physical, sexual financial and emotional abuse as well as so called 'honour' based violence and forced marriage.
- **Psychological Abuse.** This might include emotional abuse as well as threats, abandonment, humiliation, deprivation of contact e.g. with a child, bullying, isolation or withdrawal of services or support networks.
- **Financial/Material Abuse.** including theft, fraud, coercion, and misuse of the adults property.
- **Modern Slavery.** for example forced labour, trafficking, servitude and inhumane treatment.
- **Discrimination.** Including harassment, slurs, or similar treatment because of race, gender, gender identity, age, disability, sexual orientation or religion.
- **Organisational Abuse.** For example where an organisation fails to ensure proper care is provided either in a residential setting, a day centre or the adults home. This may be because of poor management, policies, processes and practices.
- **Neglect and Acts of Omission.** This could be through ignoring medical, emotional or physical care needs, failure to provide access to services and withholding the necessities of life such as medication, nutrition and heating.

- **Self Neglect.** This could include failing to care for ones personal hygiene, health or surroundings and potentially includes hoarding.

On the subject of acts of omission, a very serious national concern is that the treatment of pressure ulcers is said to cost the NHS well over a billion pounds per year. Preventing the development of pressure ulcers isn't difficult. It's largely about being alert to the risks and being effective in managing them. It is not just about reducing costs, it is also about reducing what is on the basis of that estimate, a significant source of pain and misery for a vast number of already poorly people. Regrettably it is still the case that many carers do not comprehend the risk of pressure ulcers until things have developed to a dangerous stage.

It should be noted that individuals in need of safeguarding may be subject to more than one type of abuse. Where any organisation is involved in providing their care, it is important to look beyond a single incident, as there may be evidence of multiple failures both affecting the particular adult or a number of others. To identify patterns of abuse and of course the potential for organisational abuse it is vital that information is recorded and shared with others. Patterns of abuse are all too common and are typified by;

- serial abuse in which a number of victims are groomed and abused;
- long term abuse in the context of on-going family relationships deteriorating into long term domestic or psychological abuse; and

- opportunistic abuse where valuables are routinely appropriated.

The Statutory Guidance provides detailed descriptions of each kind of abuse.

All professionals should be attentive to the welfare of carers in safeguarding concerns. Some of course might be culpable, but many others will be equally distressed by what has taken place or may themselves be at risk of harm.

Notifications and Initial Enquiries

Before reading further you should be advised that with the exception of published national performance indicators, national guidance is largely ambivalent about timescales in progressing enquiries about adult safe-guarding. This means that timescales are largely a matter of local choice as published in the procedures of the LSAB and Local Authority. In some Authority areas, there are no published timescales, these being a matter of discretion according to the individual case requirements.

The terms 'Alert', 'Notification' and 'Concern' are often used in adult safeguarding to describe points in the chain of communication to the local authority. You should check to understand how these are used to describe different activities according to local custom and practice in your area. Thus in the following very general account of activity, I have transposed these terms freely and they are likely not to describe the same activity in your particular area. The key purpose of what follows is to provide a broad description of how the process of the enquiry takes place and not a universal glossary of terms.

The objectives of enquiries are to;

- ensure the safety and well-being of the adult;
- establish the facts;
- ascertain the adult's views and wishes;
- assess the needs of the adult in terms of protection support and redress;
- Protect the adult from further abuse and neglect in accordance with their wishes;
- to consider risks to others and what might need to take place in the public interest;
- make decisions as to what follow up action should be taken; and
- enable the adult to achieve resolution and recovery.

The first priority should always be to ensure the safety and wellbeing of the adult. The adult should experience the safeguarding process as empowering and supportive.

The Local Authority is the focal point for all reports, alerts, concerns or notifications of possible abuse. In most cases these will be directed at the Local Authority Adult Social Care Service or where (where it functions in this regard) a Multiagency Safeguarding Hub (MASH – see below). Ordinarily professionals who work with the adult concerned, or family members will make such reports. However a wide range of workers and volunteers who are not explicitly responsible for personal care, are routinely in touch with people who may be at risk or suffering from abuse. These include postal and deliveries staff, meter readers, utility workers, and tradesmen. Potentially all should be vigilant for signs of possible abuse or neglect and should know what to do if they suspect it. This objective can be achieved through publicity campaigns and wherever possible, integrated into staff training.

Early and appropriate sharing of information between professionals of all agencies concerned is critical to the processes of safeguarding. To support this, all organisations should have clear and well-understood guidance for sharing information both internally and externally. Ideally, this will be underpinned through a multiagency information sharing agreement, usually led by the LSAB. Of vital importance is that no professional should be led to assume that someone else has responsibility for raising concerns. Safeguarding should be everybody's business!

In many areas, MASH have been established. There are a variety of models for MASH but in essence they exist to facilitate the timely, lawful and seamless assessment of incoming information against the wealth of information held across several agencies. Many MASH integrate chidren's and adult safeguarding functions and by doing so, ensure that risks to everyone in a family in any given situation, are properly considered.

Not all concerns justify a notification to the Local Authority. In circumstances where unintentional abuse is discovered and there is scope to remedy the situation through for example, improved training or support to a worker, a notification of a safeguarding concern to the Local Authority may not be warranted. The matter should nevertheless be recorded in such a way that it is accessible should a pattern of abuse emerge at any time in the future.

On receipt of a notification from which there is reasonable suspicion that an adult who meets the criteria for safeguarding, is, or is at risk of being abused or neglected, the Local Authority must cause enquiries to be made. These may be made by the authority's own staff or by someone else who is determined to be best placed to do so. A particular example cited in the guidance is where poor or neglectful practice has led to pressure sores; an employer-led disciplinary investigation aligned with clinical intervention, possible regulatory action and audit, may amount to a satisfactory response.

In practice, there can be a reluctance on the part of social workers to allocate enquiries back to a provider organisation due to an underlying mistrust that the enquiry might not be completed properly owing to a conflict of interest arising, i.e. mistrust of their commitment or a fear that something might be covered up.

The stark reality is that by dint of the sheer numbers of notifications that are made to Local Authorities there arises an issue of capacity. It is therefore essential that all organisations be prepared to assume responsibility for enquiries whenever it is deemed appropriate for them to do so. In any event it will usually be best for those most competent in a particular area of service to undertake the enquiries, although where circumstances warrant, consideration should be given to bringing in an independent expert.

As is the case for children, if a crime is known or suspected to have been committed, the police should be informed as well as the Local Authority. Any criminal investigation should be coordinated alongside arrangements for safeguarding.

An enquiry could be as straightforward as a conversation with the adult to determine what they would like to happen or could be a considerably more complex investigation. It should be evident that the rules of delegation apply, in that the Local Authority will always remain accountable for what takes place when an enquiry is conducted by an external agency. The Local Authority should be clear about timescales, arrangements for reporting back and what will happen if these are not complied with. Where required, the Local Authority is also responsible for appointing an advocate.

What happens as a result of an enquiry should reflect the adult's wishes, whether made by themselves or through their advocate. The exception to this being where the act of seeking the adult's views might in itself, place them at risk.

Resolution of a concern might be achieved very quickly. However the Local Authority may determine that a formal enquiry is required (S.42 Care Act 2014). This could lead to a multiagency action plan. This plan will set out how the investigation will proceed, the actions that are to be taken by each organisation involved, with clear timescales for delivery and dates for review meetings. Concurrently, other activities may be taking place and will need to be coordinated with the S.42

investigation. These could include disciplinary action, criminal investigations, Root Cause Analysis (by Health Organisations) or actions by a regulatory body such as the Care Quality Commission (CQC).

At every stage it is essential that good records are maintained of the concern, the adults wishes, action taken and the rationale for decisions. Equally important is that enquiries are handled in a sensitive and skilled way so that distress to the adult is minimised.

Following the investigation, a number of courses of action may be followed according to circumstances and consideration of the wishes of the adult(s) involved. It is usual for a multiagency planning discussion to take place at which improvement actions are agreed and prioritised. There may be several meetings of this kind during the course of the actions being completed and required outcomes achieved.

At the least there will be two tracks of actions. Firstly, those intended to keep the adult(s) and any others deemed to be at risk protected and secondly, those actions that will produce sufficient learning about what has taken place to ensure that any recurrence is prevented. Above all, these activities should be intended to deliver improvement outcomes and their effectiveness monitored through sound governance.

Special Considerations for Multiple Victims

Where the adult subject to abuse is located in a care or nursing home (a regulated setting) or where the alleged perpetrator in their role as a professional carer or nurse may be visiting a number of clients, the possibility that similar abuse might be happening to other people should always be considered from the outset.

Where abuse or neglect in a regulated setting is discovered by the employing or providing organisation, they must take steps to protect those at risk from further harm and if no conflict of interest arises, commence an investigation. In all cases they must inform the Local Authority and CQC. The Clinical Commissioning Group should also be informed if they commission services provided by the organisation.

There is no outright formula for managing enquiries or an investigation in such circumstances, as much will depend on a careful assessment of risks and how to manage them. Very often the enquiries will entail a conversation with and an assessment of, all those who might be considered to be at risk. Strategy meetings will take place involving the agencies concerned and will often include representation from the CQC. According to the management of risk, a temporary block may be placed on any further placements to a particular setting and in extreme cases, the premises might be 'deregistered' and residents rehomed elsewhere.

It is to be expected that every Local Authority or LSAB will have a policy and procedures for managing these large scale investigations.

Mental Capacity

The Mental Capacity Act 2005 (MCA) introduced substantial protections for people who are particularly vulnerable. It is estimated that around two million people in England and Wales may lack the mental capacity to make decisions for themselves. The Act created specific criminal offences relating to the ill-treatment and neglect of people who lack capacity.

Application of the MCA plays a significant part in the delivery of services, including safeguarding processes, where an adult in need of care and support is involved. The MCA will always be a consideration whenever the adult has difficulty in understanding or in communication. Note that such difficulties could be temporary or permanent. However, such difficulties must never be assumed to disbar them from active participation, choice and control. The fundamental principle here is that people must be assumed to have the capacity to make their own decisions and be given all practicable help to do so before anyone treats them as not being able to.

Where an adult is found to lack the capacity to make a decision, then any action taken, or any decision made for, or on their behalf, must be made in their best interests. Professionals and other staff need to understand and always work in line with the MCA. They should use their professional judgement and balance many competing views. They will need considerable guidance and support from their employers if they are to help adults manage risk in ways and should put them in control of decision-making wherever this is possible.

The MCA introduced a detailed infrastructure for protecting people who lack capacity embodied within the following components;

- five statutory principles;
- a test for assessing capacity;
- a legal framework of how to act and make decisions on behalf of people who lack capacity;
- attorneys who are appointed under 'Lasting Powers of Attorney';
- new Court of Protection and Court appointed deputies;
- Independent Mental Capacity Advocates;
- advance decisions to refuse treatment; and
- guidance on research on people who lack capacity.

Applying the MCA in any given circumstance requires working knowledge of the legislation. Staff who undertake an assessment of capacity and any who may take decisions in the person's best interest should have received appropriate training to do so. They will usually be the professional or carer who is directly concerned with the person at the time the decision needs to be made. For most day-to-day decisions it will be the professional or carer actually caring for them at the time the decision needs to be made. For example where a care worker or a nurse needs to assess whether a person can agree to be being bathed or to having a dressing changed.

Regular face-to-face supervision from skilled managers is essential to enable staff to work confidently and competently, especially in difficult and sensitive situations. The welfare of staff themselves should always be considered.

Mental capacity is frequently raised in relation to adult safeguarding. The requirement to apply the MCA in adult safeguarding enquiries challenges many professionals and requires utmost care, particularly where it appears an adult has capacity for making specific decisions that nevertheless places them at risk of being abused or neglected.

Deprivation of Liberty

The Deprivation of Liberty Safeguards (DoLS) are part of the MCA. They aim to make sure that people in care homes, hospitals and supported living are looked after in a way that does not inappropriately restrict their freedom.

The safeguards are designed to ensure that a care home, hospital or supported living arrangement only deprives someone of their liberty in a safe and correct way, and that this is only done when it is in the best interests of the person and there is no other way to look after them. The DoLS apply in England and Wales, but Northern Ireland (which does not have a Mental Capacity Act) has no such system in place. A deprivation of liberty authorisation cannot be used if a person has the mental capacity to make decisions, so the person's capacity will be assessed as part of the process. Note that these arrangements do not apply when someone is detained ('sectioned') under the Mental Health Act 1983.

Those planning care should always consider every option, which may or may not involve restricting the person's freedom and should provide care in the least restrictive way possible. However, if all alternatives have been explored and the hospital, care home or local authority administrating the supported living arrangements believes it is necessary to deprive a person of their liberty in order to care for them safely, then they must get permission to do this by following strict processes. These processes are the Deprivation of Liberty Safeguards, and they have been designed to ensure that a person's loss of liberty is lawful and that they are protected.

A recent Court decision has provided a definition of what is meant by a deprivation of liberty. A deprivation of liberty occurs when 'the person is under continuous supervision and control and is not free to leave, and the person lacks capacity to consent to these arrangements'. There have been several test cases in the European Court of Human Rights and in the UK that have clarified which situations may constitute a deprivation of liberty:

- a patient being restrained in order to admit them to hospital;
- medication being given against a person's will;
- staff having complete control over a patient's care or movements for a long period;
- staff making all decisions about a patient, including choices about assessments, treatment and visitors;
- staff deciding whether a patient can be released into the care of others or to live elsewhere;
- staff refusing to discharge a person into the care of others; and
- staff restricting a person's access to their friends or family.

Staff in care homes, hospitals and supported living should always try to care for a person in a way that does not deprive them of their liberty. If this is not possible, there is a requirement under DoLS that this deprivation of liberty be authorised before it can go ahead. Note that the process in supported living differs from that in care homes and hospitals (see below).

Supported living arrangements

If a person is receiving care in a supported living environment, arranged by the local authority, the Court of Protection must authorise the deprivation of liberty. This is the only route available. Anyone who feels that a deprivation of liberty in this setting may be required can ask the local authority to seek authorisation.

Care homes and hospitals

If a care home or hospital needs to provide care in a way that will deprive someone of their liberty, the registered manager of the care home, or the NHS trust or authority that manages the hospital (the managing authority) is responsible for applying for an authorisation for the deprivation of liberty. The managing authority should do this either when someone is about to be admitted, or when they are already in hospital or the care home.

The application for a standard authorisation will be made to the supervisory body. In England this is the Local Authority. In Wales this depends on where the person is receiving care for example, for care homes, the supervisory body is the Local Authority and for hospitals it is the local health board.

The supervisory body will arrange an assessment to decide whether the qualifying criteria for DoLS are met, and will either grant or refuse an authorisation.

In an emergency, the management of the hospital or care home may grant itself an urgent authorisation, but must apply for a standard authorisation at the same time. This urgent authorisation is usually valid for seven days, although the supervisory body may extend this for up to another seven days in some circumstances. Before an urgent authorisation is given, steps should be taken to consult with carers and family members.

CHAPTER FOUR

Local Safeguarding Adults Boards

> **KEY POINTS**
>
> - Local Safeguarding Adults Boards (LSAB) must be established by Local Authorities in collaboration with certain partner agencies.
> - LSABs function in a similar but not identical way to LSCBs.
> - LSABs are required to commission Serious Adult Reviews in certain circumstances.

Scope and Remit

The Care Act 2014 requires that Local Authorities must establish Local Safeguarding Adults Boards (LSAB). Their purpose is to coordinate and monitor the effectiveness of arrangements to safeguard relevant adults in their area. Safeguarding in this context means not only the processes for responding to reports of suspected abuse but also activities that contribute towards prevention. In carrying out these functions the LSAB will take an interest in a range of activities including patient safety, the quality of local support services, local provision both public and privately run, mental health services and the activities of commissioners.

Unlike the statutory requirement for LSCB, there is no requirement for an Independent Chair, although most LSABs have appointed one. The Chair is required to publish an Annual Report of the work of the Board.

Membership

In the Care and Support Statutory Guidance issued under the Care Act 2014, local NHS health services, i.e. the Clinical Commissioning Group and the Police are placed under a duty to cooperate in the establishment and running of the LSAB. A large number of other agencies are referred to in the guidance as 'relevant partners'. With regard to safeguarding, Local Authorities must cooperate with each of their relevant partners and those partners must also cooperate with the local authority in the exercise of their functions relevant to care and support including those to protect adults.

Relevant partners of a local authority include any other local authority with whom they agree it would be appropriate to co-operate (e.g. neighbouring authorities with whom they provide joint shared services) and the following agencies or bodies who operate within the Local Authority's area including;

- NHS England;
- Clinical Commissioning Groups (CCGs);

- NHS trusts and NHS Foundation Trusts;
- Department for Work and Pensions;
- Police;
- Prisons; and
- Probation services;

Local authorities must also co-operate with such other agencies or bodies as it considers appropriate in the exercise of its adult safeguarding functions, including (but not limited to);

- General Practitioners;
- Dentists;
- Pharmacists;
- NHS hospitals; and
- Housing, health and care providers.

It is usual that most if not all of these relevant partners are included in LSAB membership.

The LSAB should have a reporting regime that affords opportunities for appropriate challenge between partners that stimulates and encourages improvements and innovation. The business of the LSAB will usually be supported by a number of multiagency subgroups comprising of experts in their particular field. The work of the subgroups as well as the running of the LSAB will usually be supported by a Business Manager.

There are many similarities between the work of LSCBs and LSABs especially in terms of strategic direction and functionality. Opportunities for closer collaboration between Boards will be explored later.

Safeguarding Adult Reviews (SAR)

A LSAB must arrange for there to be a review of a case involving an adult in its area with needs for care and support (whether or not the local authority has been meeting any of those needs) if;

(a) there is reasonable cause for concern about how the LSAB, members of it, or other persons with relevant functions worked together to safeguard the adult; and

(b) condition 1 or 2 (below) is met.

Condition 1 is met if the adult has died, and the LSAB knows or suspects that the death resulted from abuse or neglect.

Condition 2 is met if the adult is still alive, and the LSAB knows or suspects that the adult has experienced serious abuse or neglect.

A LSAB may arrange for there to be a review of any other case involving an adult in its area with needs for care and support (whether or not the local authority has been meeting any of those needs).

Each member of the LSAB must co-operate with and contribute to the carrying out of a review under this section with a view to identifying the lessons to be learnt from the adult's case and applying those lessons to future cases.

The conduct of adult reviews is not subject to the same kind of regulation as those for children. This leaves it entirely to the discretion of the Board as to the particular methodology of the review and ultimately whether it should be published.

The interface with other Authority functions

Domestic Homicide Reviews

Domestic Homicide Reviews (DHR) are a statutory requirement in the Domestic Violence, Crime and Victims Act 2004 and are the responsibility of the local Community Safety Partnership (or their modern equivalent bodies). Their scope includes people living in the same household and are not simply confined to those in a relationship. These reviews often consider tragic circumstances that might also fit the criteria for a SAR or a SCR (the relevant age for DHR being 16 years and over) and thus every Local Authority will have a protocol for determining how best to coordinate reviews where this is the case.

The requirement for a DHR is triggered upon the death of a person aged 16 or over which has, or appears to have, resulted from violence, abuse or neglect by;

(a) a person to whom he/she was related or with whom he/she was or had been in an intimate personal relationship; or

(b) a member of the same household.

It should be noted that an 'intimate personal relationship' includes relationships between adults who are or have been intimate partners or family members, regardless of gender or sexuality.

A DHR may review a death arising from so called 'Honour Based Violence', 'honour crimes' and 'honour killings', which embrace a variety of crimes of violence, including assault, imprisonment and murder, where the person is being punished by their family.

The purpose of a DHR is to:

- establish what lessons are to be learned from the domestic homicide regarding the way in which local professionals and organisations work individually and together to safeguard victims;
- identify clearly what those lessons are both within and between agencies, how and within what timescales they will be acted on, and what is expected to change as a result;
- apply these lessons to service responses including changes to policies and procedures as appropriate; and
- prevent domestic abuse homicide and improve service responses for all domestic abuse victims and their children through improved intra and inter-agency working.

CHAPTER FIVE

Cross Cutting Issues for the LSCB and LSAB

KEY POINTS

- Examples of overlapping agendas are those of domestic abuse and the Government's strategy to reduce the threat of terrorism (PREVENT and CHANNEL).
- There is potential for overlapping agendas and confusion, without clear protocols or a memorandum of understanding between Boards and other statutory partnerships such as the Health and Wellbeing Board, Children's Trust and Community Safety Partnership.
- There are many opportunities for collaborative working specifically between LSAB and LSCB and also between adjoining Boards within a given region.

Abuse that Affects Adults and Children

Domestic Abuse

I make no apologies for including a relatively large section of this book on the topic of domestic abuse. My

rationale for doing so is that a substantial proportion
of children subject to child protection have become so
because domestic abuse is a feature in their lives. Many
adults at risk live in circumstances in which domestic
abuse is present and this too can be a feature of the harm
to which they may be at risk.

According to the Office for National Statistics, 1.35
million women experienced domestic abuse in 2014/15.
In 46% of cases of partner abuse, a child was present in
the household and 20% of these saw or heard the abuse
taking place. During the same period for England and
Wales, there were just short of 200,000 child protection
assessments in which social workers identified domestic
abuse as a relevant factor.

It is perhaps astonishing to reflect that up to only about
a hundred years ago, it was considered acceptable to for
a man to beat his wife. Even within the past 40 years,
public authorities were reluctant to take action or to
support women who tried to escape. What is more
astounding is that it really didn't make any difference
whether there were children associated with whatever
horrors were taking place unless there was explicit evidence that they themselves were being subjected to
physical harm.

In recent years, there have been a number of revisions
to the definition of what is considered to amount to
domestic abuse, including a new offence of exerting
coercive control. You should note that domestic violence
itself is not a criminal offence although everything that
falls within the definition will amount to a criminal act

under various legislation. The utility of the definition is to provide the parameters in which a variety of professionals and policy makers operate. The latest definition, introduced in 2013 is;

Any incident or pattern of incidents of controlling, coercive or threatening behaviour, violence or abuse between those aged 16 or over who are or have been intimate partners or family members regardless of gender or sexuality. This can encompass, but is not limited to, the following types of abuse:

- psychological
- physical
- sexual
- financial
- emotional.

Controlling behaviour encompases a range of acts designed to make a person subordinate or dependent by isolating them from sources of support, exploiting their resources and capacities for personal gain, depriving them of the means needed for independence, resistance and escape and regulating their everyday behaviour.

Coercive behaviour encompasses an act or a pattern of acts of assault, threats, humiliation and intimidation or other abuse that is used to harm, punish, or frighten their victim.

Note that this definition, includes so called 'honour' based violence, female genital mutilation (FGM) and forced marriage. It is clear that victims are not confined to one gender or ethnic group.

Recognition of the plight of children associated with domestic abuse has resulted in a significant change in legislation so that the emotional suffering of children in such circumstances is now recognised as a form of child abuse and this in turn may lead to 'child in need' or 'at significant risk of harm' processes.

Some academic studies have estimated that in 75–90% of incidents of domestic abuse, children are in the same or next room. Research arising from initial child protection conferences, has found evidence of domestic abuse in about half of all cases. Conservative estimates indicate that 30% of children living with domestic abuse are themselves subject to physical abuse. Little is known about the volume of domestic abuse perpetrated upon adults at risk, but many of those working in this field consider that it is likely to be high. Research conducted by Women's Aid has indicated that disabled women are at particular risk.

For managers of organisations whose staff may come into contact with women who are or have been subject to domestic abuse or indeed children and vulnerable adults, there should be a policy covering how staff should respond. This should include associated guidance setting out what is expected of them.

Even if staff cannot reasonably be expected to come into contact with victims of domestic abuse, there should be a policy with associated guidance for managers that covers how the organisation would respond where staff themselves may be subject to abuse. In this regard, particular consideration should be given to circumstances in which both members of a relationship work for the same organisation and also how access to a staff victim might be restricted to prevent a perpetrator abusing them in the workplace. Above all the organisation should have the welfare of any children associated with the abuse as a priority. This aspect is covered further in the section of this book covering the duties of employers.

MARAC

Multi Agency Risk Assessment Conferences (MARACs) are meetings where information about high-risk domestic abuse victims (those at risk of murder or serious harm) is shared between local agencies. Note that victims in this context include people over 16 years of age.

By bringing all agencies together at a MARAC, a risk focused, coordinated safety plan can be drawn up to support the victim. Over 260 MARACs are operating across England, Wales and Northern Ireland managing over 55,000 cases a year. Surprisingly, these are not legal entities and cooperation with MARACs is a Government expectation but not a mandatory one.

It is important to recognise that the MARAC is focused upon developing a safety plan for the victim, not their children or other vulnerable adults. If any other person is at risk of harm, they will be subject to a separate, but in most areas, a coordinated protection plan, following the child or adult protection processes outlined earlier.

Thus it will be apparent that organisations holding information about a victim or other vulnerable associated people, may be requested to provide information to support two separate albeit very important functions. Information sharing across these functions will be supported by local protocols.

All organisations should be prepared to support a MARAC and it would be best to have an internal policy as to how that should be achieved <u>before</u> receipt of any request for information, rather than have the absence of a policy become the cause of delay.

Prevent and Channel

The Prevent Strategy, published by Government in 2011, is part of the overall counter-terrorism strategy, CONTEST. The aim of the Prevent Strategy is to reduce the threat to the UK from terrorism by stopping people becoming terrorists or supporting terrorism. Often the targets of activity to radicalise, are the most vulnerable and because of this both LSCB and LSAB should be sighted on local activity in support of this important work.

Section 26 of the Counter Terrorism and Security Act 2015 places a duty on certain bodies in the exercise of their functions to have 'due regard to the need to prevent people from being drawn into terrorism'. This duty extends to schools, Local Authorities and other bodies.

The Prevent strategy has three specific objectives:

- to respond to the ideological challenge of terrorism and the threat we face from those who promote it;
- to prevent people from being drawn into terrorism and ensure that they are given appropriate advice and support; and

- to work with sectors and institutions where there are risks of radicalisation that we need to address.

Channel forms a key part of the Prevent strategy. The Channel process is a multiagency approach to identify and provide support to individuals who are at risk of being drawn into terrorism. In practice, people who are considered to be at particular risk of radicalisation may be the subject of multiagency discussion by way of a panel in which risks are assessed and mitigated through a planned programme of activities. Where vulnerable people are involved, this is likely to be coordinated with child or adult protection procedures.

Relationships and Collaboration

Health and Wellbeing Boards

The Health and Wellbeing Board (HWB) is a statutory requirement and managed by the top tier and unitary Local Authority. It is comprised of key leaders from the health and care system as well as relevant Local Authority members and officers. The aim is to work together to improve the health and wellbeing of their local population and reduce health inequalities.

HWB members will collaborate to understand their local community's needs, agree priorities and encourage commissioners to work in a more joined up way. As a result, patients and the public should experience more joined-up services from the NHS and local councils.

Boards have democratically elected representatives and patient representatives, who work alongside commissioners across health and social care in taking commissioning decisions. The boards also provide a forum for challenge, discussion, and the involvement of local people. In determining local needs, the HWB will undertake a 'Joint Strategic Needs Assessment' (JSNA) and are required to develop a joint strategy for how these needs can be best addressed. This will include recommendations for joint commissioning and integrating services across health and care. Other services that impact on health and wellbeing such as housing and education provision are also addressed.

It should be obvious that there is much potential for parallel and sometimes conflicting agendas across the work of the Local Safeguarding Children Board, the Local Safeguarding Adult Board, the Children's Trust (where such exist in a given Local Authority area), the Health and Wellbeing Board and the Community Safety Partnership (or its equivalent). The Children's and Adult Safeguarding Boards in particular, are independent legally established partnerships of their constituent agencies and are not accountable either democratically or as subservient bodies.

However, it would be extremely foolish for these bodies not to cooperate and ideally they should have strong relationships in which reciprocal challenge and opportunities for coordination and collaboration are facilitated. Most if not all Local Authorities will have established clear protocols and procedures for ensuring effective relationships. However in theory, at least, the LSCB and

LSAB exist as independent non-accountable entities. The Independent Chairs are accountable only to the CEOs of their Local Authority. Ideally, there should be arrangements for scrutiny of the work of these Boards by their constituent members, usually triggered by publication of the Chair's annual reports as well as for appraisal of the Independent Chair's performance in their role.

Similarly, there are many aspects of the work of LSAB and LSCB that lend themselves to a collaborative if not fully aligned approach. These include;

- Training and workforce development. At the service delivery interface, much of the process of protection is almost identical; albeit sometimes involving different members of the workforce. There are not only savings to be made by appropriately integrating training across both agendas, but also the potential for more thorough risk identification across a whole family rather than a focus on risk to a single individual.
- Audit and Assurance. Scrutiny of case work that considers how both adults and children are safeguarded needs to be conducted by a team comprising expertise in both domains.
- Communications. There is much potential for mixed messages where Boards have individual sub-groups managing their communications. Joining these up provides an opportunity in terms of presenting consistent and balanced information both in promoting the work of Boards and important messages to targeted groups.

- Policy and Procedures. There is a high risk that policies and procedures that are developed by separate Board subgroups, overlap or may conflict to the point that confusion at the workplace is a real possibility. At the very least there should be some collaboration and communication at the outset of policy development and ideally, relevant areas of Board business should be joined up at the point of business planning.
- Reviews. It is especially worth exploring closer collaboration where case reviews are relevant to more than one statutory partnership. This should not just be about coordinating the achievement of individual partnership objectives but on the principle of more effective learning as well as economies of scale.

Broader Collaboration

Many LSABs and LSABs, although established to have coterminous geographic boundaries with their host Local Authorities, will exist in only a part of a larger area covered by their constituent members. A good example are those Boards located within London, but this also applies to many others across the land where for example their police, health trusts, CCG, Probation Service and other agencies straddle several Boards' areas.

There is much potential for sensibly joining Boards up to cover the area served by multiple Local Authorities with the caveat only that by dint of such an exercise, the size of Board does not become unwieldy or the scope of work becomes overly broad and less effective in providing opportunities for useful challenge. Initiation of such a restructure requires real vision and determination on the part of member agencies and especially on the part of the 'host' Local Authorities who would be required to pick up most and probably all of the transitional development work.

Learning from Serious Case Reviews for Adults and Children

The most important outcome from case reviews is that learning from them is translated into improvements. It has to be said that this aspect consistently provides the greatest challenge both to realise and to evidence. Hitherto, there have been two strands of improvement planning; action plans arising from Agency Individual Management Reviews (IMR) that pertain to the single agency that conducted them and actions arising from the Overview Report that affect multiple agencies and the way that the safeguarding process straddles different services. Very often these have migrated into so called 'SMART' action plans in which the outcome intended by the IMR or Overview author often has been subverted in favour of drafting actions that are measureable.

Of course many actions lend themselves to the SMART approach and these will have the potential to be managed effectively to fruition. Regrettably some of the most important actions from reviews are not so easily addressed. This is because the particular issue that requires improvement is so deeply rooted in organisational culture, processes and practice that without significant internal commitment to change from the organisation concerned, the improvement will simply not happen.

Investigating the root causes of such failures starts in a frank discussion with practitioners. Typical examples of such a scenario are when practitioner capacity is an issue. An overworked practitioner may well as a matter of survival, opt for compromise rather than the most effective intervention. Here, the real culprit is likely to be one or a combination of factors including insupportive organisational structures, a lack of manager oversight, mistrust or less than robust supervision. Change required at this scale will affect the core business of the agency concerned and is clearly well outside the ambit of a process driven SMART action plan.

The inescapable truth is that the very process of taking change forward can easily subvert the prospects for improvement because;

- SMART recommendations have led to proliferation of tasks that do not always lead to a change in professional behaviour or interaction;
- the type of recommendations which are easiest to translate into actions may not be the ones that foster safe reflective practice;
- action plans that are easiest to implement address superficial aspects – deeper and wider issues get sidelined; and
- action on recommendations often and incorrectly implies that learning has taken place.

A useful approach to understanding the nature of the problems presented by these reviews is presented by Grint (2005) and Ritell and Webber (1973). These are described as of three types;

Critical – requires immediate intervention, needs an answer. Requires use of hierarchical power

Tame – encountered regularly, so make use of organisational procedures. Requires use of legitimate power

Wicked – The problem is ill-structured, with an evolving set of interlocking issues and constraints. There are so many factors and conditions, all embedded in a dynamic social context, that no two wicked problems are alike, and the solutions to them will always be custom designed and fitted. There may be no solutions, or there may be a host of potential solutions and another host that are never even thought of.

The nature of wicked problems is such that without a supporting infrastructure that is fit to facilitate implementation, these become too hard to do. Often they are very difficult to 'shoehorn' into SMART actions without subverting outcomes. In this context it is very easy to see how they generate barriers.

The reasons why this occurs are complex and worth exploring. The following is a list of barriers that subvert individual initiative. Some elements of this list are equally applicable to the issues that beset the implementation of solutions to 'wicked' problems. The list is not intended to be exhaustive;

- myths and previous experience e.g. that a case may not meet a threshold and therefore is not worth pursuing;
- myths about information sharing e.g. that it's unlawful;

- confused language e.g. technical language is interpreted differently by different disciplines;
- incomplete understanding of the wider family context e.g. issues affecting the capacity to parent;
- waiting for an acute incident to occur;
- only dealing with the 'here and now', not compiling information and seeing the big picture;
- lack of professional curiosity;
- not knowing the person you are dealing with from another agency;
- the collateral impact of reorganisations;
- personal anxiety and capacity and perceived absence of support;
- professional helplessness;
- organisational constraints and lack of resources;
- a natural tendency to want to keep problems tame; and
- a fear of complicating already complex dynamics.

Inherent in many of these barriers are personal attributes that amount to people being risk averse and also indicate defensiveness. Arguably these are the results of how individuals are shaped by their working environment and can be a reflection of the organisational culture in which they operate.

An important conclusion is that fundamentally, there is no flaw in the process of undertaking serious case reviews or their potential to identify areas for improvement. Systems approaches are likely to further improve the way that reviews identify problems and desired outcomes or solutions. However, the real challenge lies in the mechanisms for making these solutions happen and especially in circumstances where the problem to be resolved is identified as wicked.

Some thinking about the outcomes of a culture in which wicked problems could be solved is worthwhile here and this suggests that such a culture might be characterised by professionals who;

- were being listened to;
- felt confident;
- participated in collaborative decisions;
- were empowered to take ownership;
- were encouraged to take ownership;
- had the capacity to take ownership;
- were supported by their organisation when they took ownership;
- followed things through; and
- were recognised to be competent.

It would be easy to dismiss much of this were it not for the single inescapable fact that despite our very best efforts, time and time again, our SCRs in respect of both adults and children, identify the same mistakes being made that resulted in serious harm to someone. The principal outcome of this realisation is recognition that SMART action plans are not sufficient in themselves to achieve outcomes that require more than a process change i.e. wicked problems. Repeatedly, action plans prompt process change by way of quick wins and the really important outcomes are subverted as a result. No amount of tinkering with the nature of action planning is likely on its own to address this.

It is suggested that an environmental change needs to take place. Professionals need to be empowered to take responsibility and work together so that wicked problems can be embraced and resolved. This work needs to be owned throughout the structure and mandated and encouraged through the LSCB or LSAB. All member organisations need to support the culture change necessary for this to happen. All staff need to know that colleagues from all agencies are being encouraged to work in this way and have the support of senior and strategic management.

One approach to achieving this objective would involve a change to Local Safeguarding Board business planning to ensure that the concept of improvement through collaboration with other agencies is embedded throughout organisations and owned at strategic level. However, this cannot happen unless there is agreement from all agencies to adapt their respective organisational infrastructures. This may mean that success is measured differently and goal setting and appraisal processes may also need to change. It is essential to maintain central control as work must be focussed; however, this central control should not just concentrate on easy to quantify processes. There is a wealth of skills and experience in Local Safeguarding Boards that can contribute to this development. It is surprising to find that something like this has not already been tried.

CHAPTER SIX

What Should be in Place in your Organisation (including compliance with Section 11 Children Act 2004)

KEY POINTS

- Certain public sector organisations and those they commission for services are under a legal duty to comply with Section 11, Children Act 2004. However those that are not under such a duty are well advised to comply anyway.

- Much of what is required of organisations by Section 11 for children, is also good practice for those providing services for adults.

- A transparent trail of accountability, with routine monitoring for safeguarding children throughout the organisation is the basic building block.

- Every organisation should have clear, accessible and well publicised policies for safeguarding as well as for domestic violence.

The Duty to Safeguard

Safeguarding children and adults in need of care and support should be everyone's business, regardless of any legal obligations already placed upon them to do so. Every organisation that provides services for children and adults or that encounters children and families in the course of its operations, should as a matter of good practice apply the principles of Section 11. If for no other reason, the consequences for any organisation getting it wrong in terms of the safety of vulnerable people could be catastrophic. It is thus a matter of risk management for the organisation as well as a moral duty to protect children. Section 11 provides a useful framework that is applicable to all organisations.

However certain public organisations are explicitly under the statutory duty to safeguard and to promote the welfare of children. They are also required to ensure that any providers from whom they commission services, also safeguard and promote the welfare of children. Effectively this will amount to a contractual obligation on the part of any commissioned provider and the public organisation responsible for commissioning should actively monitor the quality of safeguarding within the operation of the contract. This means that public bodies cannot sub-contract work to avoid their responsibility under the statutory duty to safeguard and in turn, contractors have the same duty as the public body, but this will be a contractual, rather than a legal duty. Although not explicitly required by the Care Act, it would be foolish for any organisation not to include safeguarding in any contract for services to be undertaken on its behalf for vulnerable people whether child or adult.

For those Local Authorities responsible for Children's Services, the duty under Section 11 is in addition to a large number of other statutory responsibilities and duties pertaining to children and education. Specifically, Section 11 applies to;

- District Councils
- NHS bodies such as NHS England, Clinical Commissioning Groups and Hospital Trusts
- The Police
- Probation and Prison Services
- Youth Offending Teams
- Secure Training Centres
- Connexions
- State Schools and Further Education institutions.

Inexplicable ommissions from this list (even though they are subject to other external inspections and practice guidance or standards) are;

- GP Practices and other Primary Healthcare providers
- Armed Services (given that children often reside within the relatively closed community of a garrison/ base and that young people under 18 years can enlist)
- Independent Schools (although they are obliged to comply with the guidance in *Keeping Children Safe in Education*).

There are a range of other organisations for whom safeguarding is a legal responsibility, but under different legislation. These include;

- Independent Schools and colleges (not just those offering accomodation)
- Early Years Providers
- Children and Family Court Advisory and Support Service (CAFCASS)
- The UK Border Agency.

Inevitably there are a great number of commercial and voluntary sector organisations that are neither explicitly subject to Section 11 nor under a contractual obligations as a provider, but nevertheless have contact with children, vulnerable people and families. Media organisations, such as broadcasting companies, would be included here but remembering that a child includes anyone under the age of 18 years, the list also extends to employers, manufacturers, distributors, retailers, sports providers, clubs and associations. Taking a responsible approach to safeguarding adults and children should be considered a duty by all of these.

What Should be in Place

The duty to safeguard and promote welfare requires not just a broad commitment to keep safeguarding in mind in all of an organisation's undertakings. It also requires an infrastructure. The following is a summary of the requirements that appeared in the original statutory guidance to complying with Section 11 and is what could be considered to amount to a Code of Practice that all organisations should measure themselves against. At the very least, it provides a useful checklist;

1. Clear priorities for safeguarding and promoting welfare that are explicitly stated in key policy documents and in commissioning strategies.

There should be clear linkage to safeguarding in any published organisational policy and priority documents, so that the importance of safeguarding is explicit and so that all staff understand that it is a cross cutting priority. This may seem rather draconian at first sight, however many years of experience have demonstrated that unless safeguarding is lodged firmly in an organisations conciousness it rapidly becomes a marginalised aspiration... until things go wrong!

2. A clear commitment by senior management to the importance of safeguarding and promoting welfare through both commissioning and the provision of services by the organisation.

The only person who is truly accountable when safeguarding a child goes wrong is the Chief Executive. This should be explicit both to all staff and in their employment contract. It is true that to date, this accountability has not translated into a single Chief Executive being sacked. However it is only a matter of time before someone brings a lawsuit against an organisation, citing their failure to comply with Section 11 or indeed that the Chief Executive of a public body becomes subject to a criminal prosecution. If this were not sufficient incentive, the fact is that without a demonstrated commitment from senior managers running through the organisation from top to bottom, there is a significant chance that in turn the commitment of staff will rapidly erode.

3. A culture of listening to and engaging in dialogue with children and adults in need of care and support; seeking their views in ways appropriate to their age and understanding and taking account of those both in individual decisions and the establishment or development and improvement of services.

Of all the requirements in the guidance for children, this is one of the most important and probably the most difficult to accomplish. Regrettably there is not much of practical benefit that has been published in the way of supplementary guidance to help organisations to accomplish effective and truly representative engagement with children. This is frustrating because engagement with children and young people is clearly the right thing to do, is more likely to identify practical ways to deliver a service and to highlight any risks. This means that organisations need to identify WHICH children they need to engage with and HOW to accomplish this. It is patently ineffective merely to challenge a panel of volunteer children if they do not belong to the target group for services.

In my view, the key to success in this regard is the appointment of a dedicated coordinator whose role may be to solely support the organisation or shared between several, according to capacity. Such a role should be intrinsic to corporate communications not simply lodged

within safeguarding as it potentially performs a market-
ing and publicity role too.

4. A clear line of accountability and governance within
   and across organisations for the commissioning and
   provision of services designed to safeguard and
   promote the welfare of people.

All organisations from the smallest to the largest, have
a form of governance. Even if it isn't called governance
in any of them. What this looks like internally, is a
line of accountability through the organisation to the
Boardroom. There should be regular reporting and challenge to safeguarding arrangements and one member
of the Board should have reporting responsibility. The
Board should be clear about what it wants to know
so that this is not simply a 'rubber stamp' exercise.
Similarly if the local organisation is part of a national
or perhaps international body, then accountability
and governance needs to be explicit throughout. The
LSC/AB will also want to be assured about some elements of intra-organisational governance and this
should be made clear through LSC/AB meetings and in
contracts with providers.

5. Recruitment and human resources management
   procedures and commissioning processes, including
   contractual arrangements, that take account of the
   need to safeguard and promote welfare, including
   arrangements for appropriate staff checks on new
   staff and volunteers and the adoption of best practice
   in the recruitment of new staff and volunteers.

Recent statistics about registered sex offenders in England and Wales demonstrate a ratio of around 81 per 100,000 of the population. This ratio only represents those who have been caught and succesfully prosecuted; both of which functions are considerable achievements in themselves. None of us really want to admit that this horrendous perversion of human nature exists in our proximity but regrettably it really does exist everywhere and managers of organisations that recruit people who may be allowed access to the vulnerable and children should understand and take this very real risk extremely seriously.

Mitigating such risks is not straightforward. Undertaking Disclosure and Barring Service (DBS) checks is not enough on its own and in fact it is no longer possible to undertake such a check in respect of people whose only role will be in maintaining records. In any event, many paedophiles, possibly the majority, have escaped conviction. Safer recruitment will be discussed in more detail in the next chapter.

6. A clear understanding of how to work together to help keep vulnerable people, children and young people safe online by being adequately equipped to understand, identify and mitigate the risks of new technology.

This aspect on the face of things, applies only in respect of any Internet or other electronic communication access afforded to clients by virtue of the service that is provided by the organisation. Possibly the most useful approach to adopt, if this aspect is applicable to your organisation is utilisation of the self review tool provided at www.onlinecompass.org.uk/

Note that many providers including residential homes, hostels and hospitals outsource from third parties for the provision of Internet services, often as part of a package, including television. In many such arrangements, the third party establishes a direct contract with the service user. In such circumstances, the organisation that outsources the provision of these services is required to ensure that the contractor has taken steps to safeguard and promote the welfare of clients who may access these services. This is a really good example of the aspect of promoting welfare, in that access to age-inappropriate material, particularly of a sexual or very violent nature, should be restricted as part of the requirement. Outsourcing therefore is not a way to mitigate risks to the organisation, actually it may well create more risks and certainly requires additional effort in terms of governance.

Consideration should also be given to the potential for professionals employed by the organisation to become drawn into inappropriate communication with clients and especially children and this often includes the inept use of social networking. Staff should be provided with sufficient skills to manage privacy and to avoid compromising communications. These aspects are covered later, in the context of the organisation's duty as an employer.

7. There are policies for safeguarding and promoting the welfare of vulnerable adults and children, including a safeguarding policy, effective complaints procedures

and these are consistent with locally agreed inter-agency procedures as well as any other specific guidance from the Local Authority.

Every organisation that provides services for adults at risk of harm, children and families or that comes in contact with them in the ordinary course of business should have a written safeguarding policy and supporting guidance notes for how the policy should be applied. The guidance should be readily accessible to all staff. The most cursory search of the Internet will provide many examples of such policies and examples of guidance.

Most, if not all LSC/ABs have published a huge catalogue of local procedures that are based upon, but often enlarge upon relevant statutory guidance. Not surprisingly, these will be biased around the particular local nuances of service provision that exist in their local areas and so it is really important that the policies of any organisation in such a locality are in accord.

8. There are arrangements to work effectively with other organisations to safeguard and promote welfare, including arrangements for sharing information.

It may well seem from my earlier briefings about how the process of safeguarding in each domain works, that exchanging information is intrinsic to the process and should, by dint of the statutory frameworks in which it operates, be effective. Unfortunately the process relies entirely upon;

*   the knowledge and experience of those who are involved;

- that everyone who comes into contact with vulnerable people understands that safeguarding is their business and not somebody elses;
- that they know what to do when they have a concern;
- that they know who to contact when they need advice;
- that they know how to make a referral;
- ideally, they should know who it is they are speaking to; and
- they are supported by their managers.

Accountability, authority to act and a sound basis of knowledge are therefore important factors. But just as important is routine dialogue with partners at every level. This in most instances amounts to effective networking between partners, a shared appreciation of each others roles and problems and a culture of mutual support. Great examples are of regular shared lunchtime meetings between GP Practice Staff and their local Social Work Team, shared local training events such as 'managing allegations' training, local conference/training events etc. LSC/ABs are well placed to facilitate much of this.

9. Procedures for dealing with allegations of abuse against members of staff and volunteers (note this includes any allegation that suggests a member of staff or volunteer may be unsuitable to work with vulnerable people for any reason), or for commissioners, contractual arrangements with providers that ensure that such procedures are in place.

A review of internal disciplinary arrangements will establish whether these are sufficiently robust to address issues that may arise affecting the suitablity of staff to work with children. The statutory guidance issued under both the Children Act and the Care Act provides a process for managing such circumstances in a transparent way that ensures that the member of staff involved receives appropriate support and protection and that any concerns about their suitablity are properly managed and if necessary referred for inclusion in a list of people barred from working with children. One important aspect of the procedures is to ensure that people who have been subject of allegations, are not able simply to resign before the outcome of an investigation is reached and thus be at liberty to apply for another job resulting in other children being put at risk.

The requirements on organisations are usually supplemented through local procedures published by LSC/ABs. In essence they will require an appropriate senior manager from each organisation being nominated as the Designated Manager. This manager will be the conduit to the appropriate officer in their Local Authority who will determine whether a particular case meets the criteria and will agree a process for oversight of the case with the Designated Manager. In doing so a number of other agencies, especially the police, may become involved, initially to ensure that any other information about the employee that may help to determine their continued suitablility to work with vulnerable people, is included. This process has often turned up some disturbing information about employees who were previously held in high regard; including undisclosed convictions for serious crime and even false identity.

10. Arrangements to ensure that all staff undertake appropriate training to equip them to carry out their responsibilities effectively and keep this up to date by refresher training at regular intervals. All staff, including any temporary staff and volunteers should be made aware of both the organisation's arrangements and their own responsibilities for safeguarding.

At the most basic level, this means that any staff who come into contact with vulnerable people, no matter in what context, should be at least alert to the possibility of abuse and should know who in their own organisation, they should speak to if they have a concern. All staff should be provided with or have ready access to written guidance.

However those staff who actually work with adults in need of care and support or who work with children, should always maintain training at a higher level and unless the organisation already has a prescribed level of training agreed through a national professional body such as the Royal College of Nurses, then advice should be sought from the LSCB and/or LSAB. This will help to determine the most appropriate level of training, where this can be obtained and the frequency of refresher training. Additionally, a number of private sector organisations offer e-learning for staff and these include a suite of highly regarded products from organisations such as the Virtual College.

11. There are appropriate whistle-blowing procedures and a culture is fostered that enables issues about safeguarding and promoting welfare to be addressed.

Historically, the first indication of abuse in institutional settings has been when a member of staff has reported their collegues. Often in such cases they have been disbelieved by their managers or the seriousness of what was alleged has been played down. Recent high profile revelations about child sexual abuse, the activities of celebrities and the behaviour of staff in institutional setings indicate that senior managers were probably alerted to concerns by their staff and these were too readilly dismissed.

At the heart of such concerns is the very real possibility that someone is being harmed with nobody taking action to protect them. The member of staff who has made the allegation will have taken a huge risk in doing so and will be in need of support themselves. Whistle-blowing should be taken as a sign of a healthy organisation and every organisation should have a clear policy that all managers are conversant with and actively support.

CHAPTER SEVEN

Duties as an Employer

KEY POINTS

- Your staff are a valuable asset. Their selection, performance, management and welfare will inevitably impact on the quality of their work, the safety of children and the reputation of your organisation.

- Safer staff recruitment requires careful management and meticulous attention to detail, so that inappropriate individuals do not gain access to vulnerable adults or children or the records of vulnerable families.

- Legal sanctions exist against organisations that recruit staff who are barred from certain activities.

- Where there are any doubts as to the suitablity of an employee to work with vulnerable people, this should be referred for the advice of the Local Authority and local procedures followed.

- Domestic abuse affects clients as well as employees. Organisations should be clear about what managers are expected to do when it is disclosed and especially how the vulnerable are protected.

Recruiting Staff

'*For those agencies whose job it is to protect children and vulnerable people, the harsh reality is that if a sufficiently devious person is determined to seek out opportunities to work their evil, no one can guarantee that they will be stopped. Our task is to make it as difficult as possible for them to succeed.*' (Bichard Inquiry Report 2004.)

The recruitment process as well as the quality of your employment contract are critical in both ensuring that your organisation employs the best people it can find and that they are clear about the organisation's expectations of them. It is a regrettable fact however that becoming an employee of certain organisations is an extremely attractive proposition for some of the most dangerous individuals in society.

In 2012, the NSPCC obtained figures under the Freedom of Information Act, which showed there are 29,837 registered sex offenders who have committed crimes against children out of a total of 61,397 in England and Wales. Registered sex offenders are those actually convicted of a crime that is notoriously difficult to prove, especially when the only witness to the crime may be a child.

Note that the figures indicate that the number of registered sex offenders is split roughly half between those who offended against children and adults. The proportion of unregistered offenders against children is likely to be far higher. In reality, this means that there are a great deal more child sex offenders amongst the population than any official statistics can demonstrate.

An important study (Sullivan and Beech 2004), of so called 'professional perpetrators' revealed that;

- 15% chose their career solely to facilitate opportunities to abuse children;
- 41.5% said that abuse was part of their motivation for a particular choice of career;
- 77.5% had arranged meetings with children outside of work hours for the sole purpose of abusing; and
- 41.9% had established a reputation at work of being 'touchy' or 'pervy'.

These are uncomfortable statistics and we all want them not to be true. However every responsible organisation should take these facts into account and in doing so will need to take considerable care when recruiting staff who may have contact with children and their families. This much should I hope, be obvious.

However, arguably less obvious in the context of recruitment is the proliferation of paedophile networks in which information as well as images are routinely exchanged, often in return for substantial payment. This means that access to children is not the only aspect of a particular employment that may be attractive to child sex offenders and those who profit from supporting their activities.

By far the majority of adults, children and families that attract the interest of sexual predators are those already vulnerable by dint of a variety of factors, not the least of which are poverty, ignorance and low self-esteem. There is a strong trade in information about these people and especially between paedophiles through a number of networking opportunities including some that take place in prison and this is a major cause of people becoming victims of a succession of abuse by different perpetrators. Information of this kind is pure gold and the most devious will target organisations for their information about vulnerable people. Some of course will use their employment as an opportunity to befriend vulnerable families through workplace contact.

The propensity of paedophiles and other sexual predators to target the vulnerable is therefore a significant consideration. Above all many of their targets exist in a cocoon of dependency in which they instinctively respond positively to anyone apparently in authority and who seems to be supporting them. Thus they are highly susceptible to grooming and inevitably, the least likely to be believed in the event of any harm being alleged. If an organisation holds records about such people, that information is of considerable value and a substantial incentive for employment to both men and women.

The Disclosure and Barring Service

The Safeguarding Vulnerable Groups Act 2006 established the Independent Safeguarding Authority (ISA) to make decisions about individuals who should be barred from working with children and to maintain a list of these individuals. The Protection of Freedoms Act 2012 merged the ISA with the Criminal Records Bureau (CRB) to form a single, new, non-departmental public body called the Disclosure and Barring Service (DBS).

Under the Safeguarding Vulnerable Groups Act 2006 it is an offence for an employer to knowingly employ someone in a regulated activity if they are barred from doing so. It is also an offence for the individual who has been barred to apply for a regulated position. Regulated activity covers work with adults who are in need of care and support as well as children.

The Protection of Freedoms Act 2012 reduced the scope of regulated activity by focusing on whether the work is unsupervised (in which case it counts as 'regulated activity') or supervised (in which case, organisations can request an enhanced criminal records check, but this will not include a check of the barred list). The new definition of regulated activity relating to children comprises of:

(i) Unsupervised activities: e.g. teach, train, instruct, care for or supervise children, or provide advice/ guidance on wellbeing, or drive a vehicle.
(ii) Work for a limited range of establishments ('specified places'), with opportunity for contact: This does not include work by supervised volunteers.

Work under (i) or (ii) is regulated activity only if done regularly. The Government will provide statutory guidance about supervision of activity which would be regulated activity if unsupervised such as;

(iii) Relevant personal care, for example washing or dressing; or health care by or supervised by a professional.;
(iv) Registered childminding; and foster-carers.

The new definition of regulated activity came into force on 10 September 2012 and was issued in conjunction with guidance on the level of supervision required to take work out of the scope of regulated activity.

Organisations that want to request DBS checks on candidates must either:

- register with the DBS (this is only suitable for large organisations that need to carry out at least 100 checks a year); or

- use an umbrella body that is already registered with the DBS (the NSPCC is not an umbrella body). You can search for Umbrella Bodies on the Home Office website.

It is not possible for individuals to request a DBS check either on themselves or on anyone else.

Depending on the nature of the work, an employer may ask for a Standard or an Enhanced Disclosure.

Anyone working in 'regulated activity' should undergo an Enhanced Disclosure with a check against the 'barred lists' in which named individuals are subject to a legal requirement not to do certain jobs. Regulated activity includes unsupervised activities which involve regularly caring for, training, teaching, instructing, supervising, providing advice/guidance on wellbeing, or driving a vehicle for children under 18; or working for a limited range of 'specified places' with opportunity for unsupervised contact. The definitions for regulated activity are set out in the Safeguarding Vulnerable Groups Act 2006, as amended by the Protection of Freedoms Act 2012.

Enhanced disclosures should also be requested for any position where an individual has regular contact with children. However for positions outside the scope of regulated activity it is not possible to check against barred lists.

An Enhanced Disclosure will give details of convictions, cautions, reprimands and warnings held in England and Wales on the Police National Computer as well as any locally held police force information if it is 'reasonably believe(d) to be relevant', by Chief Police Officer(s), to the job role. Most of the relevant convictions in Scotland and Northern Ireland may also be included. It indicates whether the applicant is on the DBS's list of adults barred from working with children (if this has been requested).

Disclosures may not be requested for people under 16 years (for example, school children on work experience placements).

Everyone requesting DBS checks must comply with the DBS's Code of Practice to ensure that the information disclosed will be used fairly. The code also seeks to ensure that sensitive personal information is handled and stored appropriately and is kept for only as long as necessary. Disclosure checks should be stored securely and destroyed after six months.

From the information disclosed by the DBS, the organisation must decide whether the individual is suitable for the position being offered. If the information suggests that an individual might pose a risk, then the employer must undertake a detailed risk assessment before deciding whether to appoint them.

Individuals can now join the update service putting them in greater control of their information; allowing them to reuse their DBS certificates when applying for similar jobs. This will reduce bureaucracy and save them time and money.

If an individual joins the update service their employer can go online, with their consent, and carry out a free, instant check to find out if the information released on the DBS certificate is current and up-to-date.

Without this faciity, it is unwise for organisations to accept DBS checks undertaken for previous roles in other organisations without very careful consideration. This is because, new information may be known about an individual since the last check or different information may be disclosed due to the different nature of the new post.

The DBS will only issue disclosures to the applicant. Employers will need to ask the applicant to see their DBS certificate. If an individual has not shown a new certificate to their employers within 28 days of its issue, the employer may be able to request a copy from the DBS.

At the outset it should be made clear that the Disclosure and Barring Service is just one, albeit important tool and should not be relied upon as the sole determination of an employee's suitablity to work with the vulnerable.

In particular, staff whose sole responsibility involves access to records, are no longer eligible for a DBS check anyway as this is not 'regulated activity'.

At the core of any strategy to mitigate the potential of an organisation unwittingly employing such an individual, are the techniques of safer recruitment. The following should not be taken as a verbatim account of a recruitment process; that is the business of your Human Resources professionals. The following is offered as a specific guide to many additional aspects that are likely to restrict the potential for unwitting employment of a dangerous individual.

Note that any organisation that knowingly allows a barred person to work in regulated activity will be breaking the law.

There is a legal requirement on employers to refer to the DBS any information about employees or volunteers who (may) have harmed children while working for them. If you dismiss or remove someone from regulated activity (or you would have done had they not already left) because they harmed or posed a risk of harm to a vulnerable person, you are legally required to forward information about that person to the DBS. It is a criminal offence not to do so. If you believe that the person has committed a criminal offence, you are strongly advised to pass the information to the police.

Safer Recruitment

There are four stages of safer recruitment. These should be supported by a Human Resources specialist at every stage. The following is a summary and is not to be taken as an exhaustive description of the process. It should however be sufficient for managers in any organisation to recognise that recruitment in this particular context will require careful reference to the guidance provided by HM Government and referenced in the appendix at the end of this publication;

The invitation to apply

Shortlisting

References & enquiries

Interview

The invitation to apply

This should be considered as an opportunity for deterrence. The job advert should contain a clear message about the organisation's commitment to safeguarding. Any requirement for a DBS check should be made clear at the outset. Formal application forms should be used in preference to CVs. The application form should require the applicant to advise of any unspent or relevant criminal convictions and should also point out a contractual obligation to advise on any criminal investigations current or that occur during the period of employment. Failure to do so should amount to gross misconduct. This section should amount to a signed declaration by the applicant. The application form should include;

- A date of birth (to assist in verifying identity).
- Details of current employment and the reason for leaving.
- A full history since leaving school to include all employments, further education, voluntary work etc. This should show all dates of starting and leaving so that any gaps in the record can be explored.
- Qualifications and awarding body as these will need to be verified.
- At least two referees (who will be willing to speak with the prospective employer) including their contact details. If the applicant has previously worked with children, one of the references must be from that employer as well.
- A personal statement from the applicant that sets out how they meet the person specification for the job.
- A signed declaration that all of the information in the application is true. Note that it is a serious criminal offence under the Theft Act 1968 to dishonestly make a false declaration in an application for employment.

Shortlisting

This is a crucial time provided to carefully scrutinise the application. Ideally it should involve two people. Care should be taken to identify any inconsistencies and to ensure that the application is fully completed and any evidence provided relates to the person specification and job description. If the candidate is to be selected for interview, highlight any gaps, inconsistencies and concerns so as to ensure that these are explored fully if appropriate through subsequent enquiries/references and always at an interview.

References/Enquiries

Ideally, all referees should be spoken to either before any interview or if the applicant has reasonably asked this to be delayed until the outcome of the process is clear; soon afterwards. At the very least, the current or last employer and in addition if the current employment didn't involve contact with vulnerable people, any previous employer where the applicant did so. With the benefit of the Internet, telephone directories and any other networks at your disposal it should be straightforward to firstly check (i.e. before actually making contact), that the reference provided by the applicant is a genuine manager from a genuine organisation. When contact is made, you should go through the personal information supplied to ensure that the applicant and the person you will be talking about are indeed one and the same. You should always go through the referees statement with them and clarify any ambiguities.

Ask the following questions of the referee and make a record of their responses;

- whether the referee is aware of any behaviour that might give rise to any concern;
- whether there were any allegations specifically in terms of the applicants behaviour towards a vulnerable person;
- whether they were subject to any disciplinary action;

- Confirm the duties and responsibilities of the post they held and the dates of their employment; and
- always fully explore any inconsistencies or ambiguities with the referee.

Of perhaps greater importance than any reliance upon checks is the maintainance of a safe culture within the workplace that ensures that all staff are aware of what they should do when they think someone may be being abused and feel empowered to report their misgivings to someone senior who will take them seriously.

Interviews

All organisations that provide services to children should actively engage with children so that the child's perspective is included in the development of those services. This is a serious commitment and includes having children involved in the recruitment process. Many organisations have already built arrangements for children to be engaged in their recruitment processes and it is truly shameful that many, especially public bodies, have not. This is not about tokenism. Children appropriately engaged in a recruitment process can offer a unique perspective on the qualities of an applicant that can positively enhance the process. This includes shortlisting. Similarly, the views and concerns of vulnerable adults should be considered.

Serious consideration should be given to the use of screening interviews. The purpose of such an interview is to explore many sensitive personal issues in order to ensure a candidates suitability to work with children.

The screening interview should always involve at least two interviewers. The interview should be used; (i) to ensure that the candidate has a full understanding of the job requirements and challenges and (ii) to explore how the candidates life experience has enabled them to develop necessary qualities, skills and aptitudes for the job. The process of conducting the screening interview should include an exploration of any gaps in the employment record and especially any vagueness, a probe of the candidates attitudes and their motivation for working with the vulnerable and to probe for any prejudices and discrimination.

The applicant should bring originals of their birth certificate or passport and at least two utility bills showing their address. If a passport is not produced, a driving license or other form of photographic identity should be made available. Do not be afraid to seek further documentation if there is any doubt as to the validity of evidence to prove that the applicant is indeed the person they claim to be. You should also ask to see originals of qualifications, professional registration and other relevant documents. Above all, be curious and never accept anything at face value. It is extremely easy using desktop publishing to falsify any amount of very professional looking documents.

For further information about safer recruitment please refer to your LSCB website where training may also be available. The Department for Education have published guidance 'Recruiting Safely: Safer recruitment guidance helping to keep children and young people safe'.

Specific arrangements for managing allegations against people who work with children and adults at risk.

At the outset, you should note that although the following describes the processes affecting children, many LSABs have adopted similar procedures for people who work with adults at risk. In both cases you should consult your local LSAB and LSCB procedures as there may be variations.

Since the tragic events that took place in Soham, a procedure has been developed to manage the circumstances in which an allegation is made or a concern arises that suggests that an employee may not be suitable to work with children. The procedure has been necessary to ensure that where such a concern arises it is used as a trigger for close cooperation between agencies so that any additional information held by others is factored into the inquiry and to provide multiagency assurance that children are not put at risk by dint of the employee continuing to have inappropriate access to children in that or any other future employment.

Note that this procedure does not just cover circumstances in which the professional has actually harmed a child or adult at risk, it may include those in which ignorance, incompetence, their conduct, or their prejudice affects the way that the professional behaves and in doing so may present a risk to a particular child or adult at risk or indeed others whom they may come into contact with. Specifically, the procedure covers cases in which it is alleged that a person who works with children or adults at risk has;

- behaved in a way that has harmed them, or may have harmed them;
- possibly committed a criminal offence against or related to a child or adult at risk; or
- behaved towards children or adults at risk in a way that indicates s/he is unsuitable to work with them.

It should be noted at the outset that this procedure is applied in addition to any internal diciplinary procedures operated by the employing organisation. Therefore there may be up to three strands in consideration of such an allegation;

- a police investigation of a possible criminal offence;
- enquiries and assessment by social care about whether a child or adult at risk is in need of protection or services; and
- consideration by an employer as to disciplinary issues.

In this particular context the term employer is used to cover any organisation that has a working relationship with the individual against whom the allegation is made. This includes organisations that use the services of volunteers, or people who are self-employed. Where an employment agency may be involved, both the parties to any contract are deemed to be employers and will need to cooperate in the progress of dealing with the allegation.

For children, the Local Authority are required to appoint a specified officer, often referred to as a Local Authority Designated Officer (LADO) who is responsible for recording and coordinating progress of the allegation. The same or a similar post may be established to manage allegations against people who work with adults at risk.

To that end, the LADO will be available to offer advice to any organisation that raises a concern about a particular individual. Very often the LADO may discern at an early stage that the procedure is not warranted in the circumstances. This will be after the LADO has ensured that nothing else is known about the employee by other relevant agencies. However it is the absolute duty of organisations to report all concerns to the LADO in the first instance and not to 'second guess'.

Every LSCB member organisation is required to appoint a senior manager (the designated liaison officer) whose role is to manage the interface between their organisation and the LADO. They should also have a nominated 'deputy' to act in absentia. Ideally there will be the same or a similar post in respect of adults at risk.

For a host of practical reasons it is best that such a manager is directly linked to internal processes for managing complaints or disciplinary procedures affecting employees. This ensures that the line of internal communication is not unduly protracted. It is unlikely that safeguarding professionals would be well placed within their organisations to fulfill such a role, although should be consulted when their specialist expertise is likely to be useful.

Most, if not all LSCBs offer training for Designated Managers and this training also offers the opportunity to meet with the respective LADO.

It should be understood that the procedure ensures that the progress of any allegation of this kind is properly monitored by the LADO and;

- that arrangements for the safety of any children or adults at risk involved are confirmed to be in place;
- that no so called 'compromise agreements' are reached in which for example, the employee is allowed to resign in lieu of the allegation being properly tested;
- that the person subject to the allegation is properly supported;
- that where appropriate, any parents or carers of children or adults at risk directly affected by the allegation, are kept informed

The Procedure

If an allegation is made to the police, the officer who receives it should report it to the Force Designated Liaison Officer without delay and in turn the designated liaison officer should inform the LADO straight away. If the allegation is made to someone in a Local Authority, the person who receives it should inform the respective LADO without delay. All other organisations that receive such an allegation or concern should inform their Designated Manager immediately, who in turn should make contact with the LADO within a working day.

The LADO will obtain full particulars of the allegation from the employer and consider the weight of evidence to determine whether it might be false or unfounded. If the allegation is not patently false and there is cause to suspect that a child or an adult at risk may be at risk of significant harm, the LADO will immediately refer to Social Services to initiate a strategy discussion and the protection process outlined relevant to whether a child or adult at risk is involved. Ordinarily such a discussion will include the LADO and employer's representative. If there is no cause to suspect significant harm but there is the possibility of a criminal offence, a similar discussion should be initiated involving the police and again a representative of the employer should be present.

Where initial evaluation does not involve the possibility of a criminal offence, the investigation will be dealt with by the employer. If the nature of the allegation does not require formal disciplinary action, appropriate action must be instituted within three working days. If a disciplinary hearing is required and can be held without further investigation, this should take place within 15 working days.

Where further investigation is required to inform consideration of disciplinary action, the employer should discuss who will undertake this with the LADO. In some circumstances it may be necessary to appoint an independent investigator. In any case the investigating officer should report to the employer within 10 working days. On receipt of the investigation report, the employer should within two working days, decide whether a disciplinary hearing is required If a hearing is required, this should take place within 15 working days.

When considering whether a hearing is required, the employer should take into account any relevant information arising from any Social Services enquiries to determine whether the child or adult at risk is in need of protection. There should be routine and effective communication between the LADO and the Designated Manager throughout.

At the conclusion of any investigation, the LADO will be required to consider whether referral to a relevant professional body or the Disclosure and Barring Service is appropriate. If so, such a referral must be made within one month. A referral must always be made if the employer thinks that the individual has harmed a child or poses a risk of harm to children and I suggest this should be the same for any adult at risk as well.

Culpable Individuals

Where, as a result of a review or other process, any individual is deemed culpable through acts of deliberate abuse or neglect, criminal proceeding may be considered. However, the standard of proof for prosecution in criminal courts is 'beyond reasonable doubt' and this sets the bar for a conviction at a very high and often unachievable level.

The standard of proof for internal disciplinary procedures and for discretionary barring consideration by the Disclosure and Barring Service (DBS) is usually the civil standard of 'on the balance of probabilities'. This means that when criminal procedures are concluded without action being taken or where an alleged perpetrator is not convicted of an offence, this does not automatically mean that regulatory or disciplinary procedures should cease or not be considered. In any event there is a legal duty to make a safeguarding referral to the DBS if a person is dismissed or removed from their role due to harm to a child or a vulnerable adult.

Domestic Abuse; your employees and children or adults at risk in their care

Domestic Abuse – Issues for Managers to Consider

- Domestic abuse is a significant national issue and it is estimated that one in four women will be victims in their lifetime.
- Men are victims as well as women.
- It is for the individual to recognise that they are a victim of domestic abuse and it should be entirely their own decision as to whether to take action or to seek support, if they have capacity.
- Overriding all other considerations, if any children are suspected to be in need or at risk, staff must comply with the LSCB Inter Agency Child Protection Procedures with a view to making a referral to Local Authority Children's Services and if appropriate, should seek advice from a senior manager.
- The effects of domestic abuse can be wide-ranging and people experience it regardless of their social group, gender, age, ethnicity, marital status, disability, sexuality or lifestyle. In particular, domestic abuse has significant health implications including serious injury, exacerbation of other medical conditions, stress and mental illness.
- The legal obligations, on any organisation, include the duties within the Human Rights Act 1998 and

European Convention on Human Rights to protect life and to protect individuals from inhuman and degrading treatment.

- Appropriate partnership working with criminal justice agencies and other statutory and voluntary sector services is essential. Where relevant, your organisation should facilitate full participation in Multi Agency Risk Assessment Conference (MARAC) arrangements.
- All employers have a responsibility to provide a safe and healthy working environment for their staff. Domestic abuse can affect an individual's work performance.
- Line managers and colleagues should be aware of signs that may indicate that an employee may be a victim. Posters and information in a variety of formats should be displayed in prominent places throughout the workplace.
- Managers should be able to provide information to ensure an employee seeking help has immediate access to professional assistance. This information will include appropriate aid agencies, the police, local refuges and help lines and specialist organisations.
- Employees should be encouraged to talk to their line manager, but it is recognised that they may not wish to do this.
- To allow for an informal approach for advice and guidance, staff should be directed to a named employee who may be a union or other representative.
- Where possible, the victim should have access to help from someone of the same sex, sexual orientation or age as himself or herself. It is also important that the contact and those managers involved have received training.

- It should be remembered that dealing with a colleague who is the victim of domestic abuse might be distressing for employees. They may also need support.
- Any employee who is concerned about a colleague should talk to their line manager in the first instance.
- Special paid leave should be provided for appointments where necessary. Examples of this provision would be for counselling, visits to support agencies, solicitors, court, for re-housing or to alter childcare arrangements. Other requests for paid leave and extended unpaid leave should be considered sympathetically. No records of the specific reasons for such absences should be held on the employee's file.
- Periods of absence, including sickness absence, should not have an adverse impact on the employee's employment record where they arise from domestic violence and abuse.
- Requests for advance of pay should be considered sympathetically as should requests for pay to be flexibly paid across different bank accounts to assist the victim to become financially independent.
- Flexible working arrangements may assist an employee in this situation, and should also be given sympathetic consideration.

Domestic abuse is a serious matter that can lead to criminal convictions. Employees should be aware that conduct outside work might lead to disciplinary action against an employee who is perpetrating domestic violence and abuse because it undermines the organisation's confidence in them and is likely to harm the employer's reputation. Terms and Conditions of Employment should require all employees to conduct themselves in a professional manner at all times and to comply with conditions pertaining to any professional registration. All employees should be required to notify their managers immediately when arrested, charged or convicted of any criminal offence. A conviction for domestic violence and abuse could be considered to have brought the organisation into disrepute.

Situations where both the victim and the alleged perpetrator work for the same organisation, or where a victim of domestic violence needs to access services at a location where the alleged perpetrator is employed, need to be handled particularly sensitively. Ensuring safety for the victim and any relevant colleagues in the workplace may involve the suspension or redeployment of the alleged perpetrator pending a disciplinary investigation.

- Misuse of workplace information and resources to continue abuse, should be deemed to be bringing the company/organisation into disrepute and dealt with as a disciplinary offence.
- Perpetrators should be supported in finding help.
- Information about domestic abuse and the organisation's policy should be made available to all employees and service users in a way in which they can understand it.

Appraisals

Safeguarding should be included as an aspect of staff appraisal. At the most basic level, this should act as a triangulation point to ensure that relevant training is up to date, supervision has been taking place and to identify future training needs. This is also an opportunity to test the outcome of any training received and especially whether any change in practice has resulted.

Welfare and Supervision

For the majority of organisations, employees are a substantial and critically important resource. Mention has already been made of the emotional impact that can be incurred through working with children and vulnerable adults. Thisimpact rarely takes place in isolation and is often in the context of dysfunctions within the child's family and any personal anxieties arising from the employee's personal circumstances. Furthermore, it is literally true that no two families are the same; each present their own unique suite of issues that challenge even the most resilient of practitioners.

In health and social care organisations, regular clinical supervision is a standard feature of employment in which a confidential review of cases takes place. This is aimed to identify improvements in practice for the benefit of all. This practice often identifies welfare concerns such as stress and particularly any that might be affecting the quality of engagement with families.

People who are working with vulnerable adults, children and familes deserve the support of their organisations and this includes routine engagement with their managers and peers in a supportive way that encourages them to disclose anything that might affect the quality of their work.

The Social Care Institute for Excellence emphasises how effective supervision is a key component in staff management, which can lead to the following improvements:

- Greater individual motivation
- Understanding of how work links into overall objectives
- More effective time management
- Ability to plan workload
- More effective coordination of work
- Better two-way communication
- Reduction in conflict/misunderstanding
- Learning on the job
- Reduction in stress levels.

Support and supervision sessions are regular one-to-one meetings where work performance is discussed in a systematic manner. The session takes the form of a semi-structured interview with the emphasis on encouraging dialogue between the manager and the member of staff.

Support and supervision is concerned with monitoring work in hand, reviewing progress against individual work plans, discussing problems, developing solutions, and delegating new tasks and projects. Effective support and supervision should maximise learning on the job and support the individual in a way which is appropriate to their stage of development. The wider process of reviewing overall performance and managing personal and career development are best considered as part of a systematic staff appraisal system, although this is a parallel and complimentary management process.

Effective supervision and support will generally cover four broad areas:

- Review of work
- Delegation of tasks/projects
- Priority setting
- Training and development review.

It should cover both the regular work of employees and other activities such as attendance at various task groups, networks, etc.

For further reading, I heartily recommend a book by the late Tony Morrision; *Strength to Strength A facilitator's guide to preparing supervisees, students and trainees for supervision. ISBN 978 1 84196 175 0*

CHAPTER EIGHT

Management in Context

KEY POINTS

- The first step to identifying what needs to be done is to review arrangements within the organisation against the learning from this book and associated references.
- There should be high level support for the review and it's outcomes, accountability for completion with a realistic timescale for completion.
- Expert advice should be sought from any specialists within the organisation or via the LSAB and LSCB.
- Completion of the review should trigger a programme of improvements that is supported by and routinely monitored by the organisation's Executive Board.

The Functions of Management

The functions of management have been described as;

- planning;
- organising;
- implementing and
- controlling.

None of these functions can take place without a sound understanding of what is in place and what needs to be done. In the context of safeguarding children, a first step to planning what needs to be done, is to consider undertaking the review of what what is currently in place and setting this in the context of what should be.

How to Undertake a Review of your Organisation

The body of this publication will provide you with a useful insight into what should be in place. However a useful checklist from which to explore further is provided under the headings of;

- Accountability
- Policy and Procedures
- Staff Recruitment and Training
- Record Keeping
- Performance Information.

This list is not exhaustive. The content will inevitably vary from one type of organisation to another. It is hoped that the following will at the very least provide a starting point.

Accountability

- Is the line of accountability clear to everyone in the organisation?
- Is it clear that the Chief Executive of the organisation is ultimately accountable?
- Is safeguarding a matter of routine (at least annual) scrutiny by the Executive Board?
- Does this scrutiny include an analysis of performance information (see below) pertinent to safeguarding activity?
- Is a member of the Board (i.e. at the level of Director or equivalent) personally responsible to the Board for safeguarding operationally?
- Is a senior manager nominated as a Designated Liaison Officer for Managing Allegations?
- Is there a deputy for this role available to act in absentia?

Policy and Pocedures

- Does the organisation have an explicit and accessible policy in place for safeguarding?
- Is the policy subject to periodic review? By whom?
- Is the policy subject to approval at Board level?
- Does the organisation have a domestic violence and abuse (DVA) policy (this may be included in other Human Resource policies).
- Does the DVA policy explicitly discuss the action to be taken where children may be affected?
- Is safeguarding a matter of routine discussion at workplace meetings, particularly those in which service user concerns are discussed?
- Where a disclosure/suspicion of a safeguarding concern or DVA arises, is this considered in respect to risks presented to other family members?
- Where a child is subject to a child protection plan and is referred to another agency/specialist, are there arrangements to ensure that the other agency or specialist is made aware of the fact of the CP Plan and the name of the relevant Children's Services worker?
- When a child or a vulnerable adult misses an appointment, this should be followed up.

Staff, Awareness and Training

- Are the principles of safer recruitment included in recruitment processes?
- Is safeguarding training mandatory for specific staff groups?

- Are all staff who may come into contact with children or vulnerable adults provided awareness training of what to do when they think that someone is being abused, on induction or soon afterwards?
- Does the organisation have systems to identify which staff should be trained in safeguarding at a higher level than basic awareness?
- Is the training at any level available in a timely way and accessible for all relevant staff?
- Have the Designated Liaison Officer and Deputy received training in Managing Allegations?
- Is there acceptable compliance with training at any level provided? (Suggested 90% or higher for most organisations. (Note that this would account for staff turnover.)

Records

- Are personal records of vulnerable adults, children and their families capable of being 'flagged' to allow for identification by appropriate professionals of people considered to be at risk of harm or those subject to protection?
- Can family members be readily linked across records, even though they may not live at the same address?
- Are disclosures of domestic abuse recorded? How?
- Are all entries timed and do they show the identity of who made them?
- Are any arrangements for record keeping compliant with Data Protection Legislation and any other pertinent rules of confidentiality to the organisation?

- Are all referrals and any other concerns recorded in such a way as to illuminate staff workloads as well as to monitor the timeliness of reports and outcomes?

Performance Information

It is vital that resources are allocated on the basis of evidence rather than instinct. In this regard, safeguarding should not be an exception. This means that information about resources, activity and caseloads should be readily available and capable of interpretation. These should be monitored frequently at the level of line managers and at least monthly at a more senior level. An analysis of the data should be presented to the organisation's Management Board at least annually. Most of the issues subject to the review process outlined above would lend themselves to a variety of useful indicators.

However by far the most challenging aspect of performance is that of measuring staff capacity and the potential for catastrophic overload. There are no tailormade formulae that can be applied across all organisations or for that matter similar ones.

A single member of staff may be able to manage a large number of complex cases in one scenario and another working in a more intensive provision may be overwhelmed by a small number of similar cases. The most important point to be made here is that this is not an area in which to 'fly by wire'. It should be a priority for managers to determine an acceptable caseload formula based upon the type and nature of cases through consultation with staff and their respective unions/professional bodies. By that means, and only by that means, can risks associated with staff overload be properly assessed and managed. It is a salutory fact that in my experience, too few organisations have attempted this seemingly obvious piece of work and as a result seem to rely solely upon staff absenteeism and resignations as the only clues to an impending disaster.

Conclusion

The most important step that any manager can take in establishing a safe organisation is to undertake a review of what is in place against the advice contained in this book. This will provide the necessary evidence to support the kinds of critical changes that will make yours a safe organisation. Above all else, the establishment of high level monitoring that provides a true insight as to the way your organisation safeguards vulnerable people is of vital importance.

At the most basic level, the list outlined previously in the chapter can be used as the framework for such a review. Ideally, those staff who already have some experience of safeguarding within the organisation should be consulted for their advice as to other relevant issues that should be included.

A further useful source for compiling the content of a review can be obtained from the LSCB. The majority if not all LSCBs conduct periodic audits of member organisations to determine the extent of compliance with Section 11 Children Act 2004. A similar exercise is conducted by most LSABs. It would be useful to any organisation subject to such an audit, to factor the audit framework into their own internal review not just as an economy of scale but also because it should reflect particular local circumstances and concerns.

FURTHER READING

Supplementary guidance on particular safeguarding issues; all which can be found on the Internet;

Children

Working Together to Safeguard Children (2015), https://www.gov.uk/government/publications/working-together-to-safeguard-children—2

Safeguarding children who may have been trafficked, https://www.gov.uk/government/publications/safeguarding-children-who-may-have-been-trafficked-practice-guidance

Safeguarding children and young people who may have been affected by gang activity, https://www.gov.uk/government/publications/safeguarding-children-and-young-people-who-may-be-affected-by-gang-activity

Safeguarding children from female genital mutilation, http://www.education.gov.uk/childrenandyoungpeople/safeguardingchildren/a0072224/safeguarding-children-from-female-genital-mutilation

Forced marriage, http://www.education.gov.uk/children andyoungpeople/safeguardingchildren/a0072231/ forced-marriage

Safeguarding children from abuse linked to faith or belief, http://www.education.gov.uk/childrenandyoung people/safeguardingchildren/a00212811/safeguarding-children-from-abuse-linked-to-faith-or-belief

Use of reasonable force in schools, http://www.education. gov.uk/aboutdfe/advice/f0077153/use-of-reasonable-force

Safeguarding children and young people from sexual exploitation, http://www.education.gov.uk/childrenand youngpeople/safeguardingchildren/a0072233/ safeguarding-children-from-sexual-exploitation

Safeguarding Children in whom illness is fabricated or induced, https://www.gov.uk/government/publications/ safeguarding-children-in-whom-illness-is-fabricated-or-induced

Preventing and tackling bullying, http://www.education. gov.uk/aboutdfe/advice/f0076899/preventing-and-tackling-bullying

Keeping Children safe in Education, https://www.gov. uk/government/publications/keeping-children-safe-in-education—2

Information sharing for safeguarding practitioners, https://www.gov.uk/government/publications/safe guarding-practitioners-information-sharing-advice

What you need to know about Early Help, http://www. local.gov.uk/c/document_library/get_file?uuid=50e 58128-e1e3-4e66-bfaa-7cdd852a98d8&group Id=10180

Recruiting safely: The Disclosure and Barring Service, https://www.gov.uk/government/organisations/ disclosure-and-barring-service

Safeguarding Disabled Children: Practice guidance, https://www.gov.uk/government/publications/safe guarding-disabled-children-practice-guidance

Adults

Care Act – Care and Support Statutory Guidance, https:// www.gov.uk/government/publications/care-act-2014-statutory-guidance-for-implementation

Making Safeguarding Personal, http://www.local.gov. uk/adult-social-care/-/journal_content/56/10180/ 6074789/ARTICLE

Mental Capacity Act – making decisions, https://www. gov.uk/government/collections/mental-capacity-act-making-decisions http://www.scie.org.uk/publications/ ataglance/ataglance43.asp

Children and Adults

Revised Prevent Duty Guidance, https://www.gov.uk/
government/uploads/system/uploads/attachment_data/
file/445977/3799_Revised_Prevent_Duty_Guidance__
England_Wales_V2-Interactive.pdf

Channel Duty Guidance, https://www.gov.uk/govern-
ment/uploads/system/uploads/attachment_data/
file/425189/Channel_Duty_Guidance_April_2015.pdf